Burncourt

A History

Burncourt

A History

Rose M. Cleary

Eastwood

First published by Eastwood Books, 2019
Dublin, Ireland

www.eastwoodbooks.com
www.wordwellbooks.com
@eastwoodbooks

First Edition

Eastwood Books is an imprint of The Wordwell Group

Eastwood Books
The Wordwell Group
Unit 9, 78 Furze Road
Sandyford
Dublin, Ireland

ISBN 978-1-9161375-5-4

British Library Cataloguing in Publication Data.
A catalogue record for this book is available from the British Library.

Typeset in Ireland by Wordwell Ltd
Copy-editor: Myles McCionnaith
Cover design and artwork: Eastwood
Printed by: Digital Print Dynamics

Contents

Acknowledgements

The preparation of this book was facilitated by a number of individuals and the author wishes to credit the following: Roísín O'Grady, Heritage Officer, Tipperary County Council and Tipperary Council, for a subvention towards the cost of publication; Myles McCionnaith for trojan editorial work to bring the initial draft to a publishable standard; Ronan Colgan, of Eastwood Books and the Wordwell Group; Alice Mulcahy for information and discussion of the War of Independence; Neil Donovan for information on local Volunteers during the War of Independence; William Mulcahy for useful information on past farming practices, folklore and place names. Also, thanks to the following for the pictures: Tony O'Brien, book cover photographs; Jimmy Fitzgerald (Fig. 3); Ed O'Riordan (Fig. 29); Leonard Godsil (Figs 43–44); Paul Buckley (Fig. 58), Maureen Creed (Figs 62–63) and Breda McGrath (Fig. 66).

1

Introduction

BURNCOURT is a rural area and part of the larger ancient parish of Shanrahan, now Burncourt and Clogheen. The name 'Burncourt' derives from the burning of the Everard Mansion in 1650. This was done either by Oliver Cromwell or, as local lore has it, by Lady Catherine Everard, who did not want the castle to fall into Cromwellian hands. The castle was never reoccupied and now lies as an imposing ruin on the landscape. Burncourt is an area where history abounds, yet we will never know the full story of the place. This book takes a brief look at how the area developed and evolved into what is Burncourt today, and how the landscape was shaped by past events. At best, all that can be provided are glimpses into the past. Prominent historical persons including Lord Inchiquin, Cromwell, Geoffrey Keating, Nicholas Sheehy, Bishop John Brenan, the Sugán Earl and the White Knight came to Burncourt. History shapes a community and a community can shape the spirit of a place. This is Burncourt.

The story of Burncourt begins in the landscape setting on the north side of the valley between the Galtee and Knockmealdown Mountains. The Mitchelstown caves are one of the better-known landscape features, the new caves being discovered in 1833. This network of underground caverns has a place in history where the Sugán Earl hid after the Munster Rebellion and was ultimately hounded down in 1600. The caves also have a strong place in the folklore of the area.

There is little evidence of prehistoric settlement in the area; the earliest tribe recorded in the area were the Déisi, who controlled much of South Tipperary and Waterford. This tribe were in contact with Britain, and it is through this that early Christianity came to Munster, probably before St Patrick began to preach and Christianise the northern part of Ireland. The Déisi were expelled from the territory by the Eóganachta Cashel and these in turn were overtaken by the Dál Cais around AD 900. After the Norman invasion in 1166, the area around

1

Burncourt was under the control of the Butlers, Everards and Fitzgeralds; Fitzgibbons (White Knights), a scion of the Fitzgeralds, also owned lands in South Tipperary. The Everard lands were eventually acquired by the O'Callaghans of Lismore in 1721. The O'Callaghan's lived in the area and ultimately built Shanbally Castle.

One of the earliest buildings in Burncourt is the medieval church at Ballysheehan, which was on the site of an ancient church. The church building that survives was built in the fourteenth century and supported by Norman landowners, who introduced the parochial system into Ireland. The surrounding graveyard has memorial stones which chart the history of the dead from the early eighteenth century to modern times, and the family names as well as descendants still survive in the Burncourt area.

Burncourt Castle was built in the 1630s and Sir Richard Everard moved to Burncourt in 1641. His new house was more of a mansion house than his former home in the cramped castle at Ballyboy. He was an improving landowner and sought to better his estate management. He brought in English tenants who were skilled in what were then superior farming techniques. Sir Richard had only just arrived at Burncourt Castle when the 1641 rebellion broke out and he had to move eighty-eight tenants into the castle grounds for their safety. This was not an auspicious start in his new home. The castle was attacked by Lord Inchiquin in 1648 and Lady Catherine Everard had to flee, although she returned under the protection of the Duke of Ormond. Cromwell took the castle in January 1650 and either he or Lady Catherine set it on fire.

The Penal Laws, imposed on Ireland from around 1700, saw strict laws enforced relating to the practice of the Catholic religion. Mass attendance was in secret, hence Mass paths came into use which led to sites where Mass was said in secret. Schooling was also forbidden and hedge schools provided basic education. Burncourt, in Penal times, saw Bishop John Brenan minister in the area, where there was a lack of clergy and resources. The Penal era was one of troubled times, as small landholders were displaced from their farms. There was also the imposition of tithes, or taxes, to support Protestant clergy. The Whiteboy movement spearheaded resistance to these developments. Fr Nicholas Sheehy emerged as a champion of the poor and dispossessed. He was charged with sedition and falsely accused of murder; he paid the ultimate price and was hanged, drawn and quartered in Clonmel in 1766. The pattern of evictions continued into the early nineteenth century when landowners, including Viscount Lismore of Shanbally, the Buckleys of Galtee Castle and the Charteris of Cahir, who all held land around Burncourt, forced small farm tenants off their lands, moving the dispossessed to the slopes of the Galtee Mountains in order to make bigger farms on their estates. This farmland skirted the new road (the 'Top Road'), which was built in 1794.

Burncourt and the surrounding lands were part of at least three main estates. The O'Callaghan landowners (later Viscount Lismore) owned property extending south to Clogheen as far as the Galtee Mountains. Cornelius O'Callaghan built a large house at Coakley's Cross around 1735–41 and was created Baron Lismore. His descendant, also Cornelius O'Callaghan, who was Viscount Lismore, completed Shanbally Castle in 1812. The Butler estate, (later the estate of the Earl of Glengall and, from 1858, the Charteris estate) extended as far as the north-east of Burncourt and included Rehill while the Kingston estate (later the Buckley estate) included some of the north and west side of Burncourt. Many of the roads around Burncourt were made around 1791–95. These roads facilitated commerce and enabled the landlords to bring farm produce to markets. The 'Top Road', or former N8, linked Cahir to Mitchelstown and the Earl of Glengall's estate in Cahir to Kingston's in Mitchelstown as well as the Shanbally estate around Burncourt.

Famine struck Tipperary in 1845 and the effects were catastrophic for both tenants and landlords. The Famine worsened in 1846–48, with a huge loss of life and a loss to the country through emigration. It was also a disaster for landlords, as tenants were unable to pay rents. The farms on the foothills of the Galtee Mountains were hardest hit; the population dropped by up to 60 per cent on some of them. Potato ridges can still be seen along the lower mountain slopes. Evictions from the better lowland continued after the Famine and the poor continued to be dispossessed. An account by William O'Brien regarding conditions on the Galtees was published in the *Freeman's Journal* in 1878 and depicts a population suffering poverty and near-starvation. Failure to pay ever-increasing rents resulted in eviction and destitution.

One bright aspect of community life in Burncourt was the building of the national school in 1841–42. The archives for the school show that there was huge local support for education and money was raised from what was essentially the poor to build the school. Burncourt National School is the oldest school in the area. The building was later bought by the community in the late 1970s and converted into a community centre. A new school was built in 1956. A church was built around 1812 and renovated in 1874. This was replaced in 1952 by the present church.

While the battlefields of World War I may seem remote from Burncourt, the war saw the loss of a number of young men from the area. Private William Anderson of the Royal Fusiliers lived in Rehill Wood and was killed in action in July 1916, aged 21 years. Sub-Lieutenant Adrian Maloney, from Old Shanbally, died on the Western Front at the Somme in 1918. Kit Conway also joined the British Army but feigned insanity and was discharged. Kit Conway fought in the War of Independence (1919–21) as part of the 3rd Tipperary Brigade and later joined the No 2 Flying Column under the direction of Seán Hogan. He fought fearlessly on the Republican side in the Spanish Civil War (1936–39) and was killed at the Battle of Jarama on 12 February 1937.

The local Volunteers formed in 1914 and were part of the 6th Battalion of the 3rd Tipperary Brigade under the direction of Seán Treacy. When the first shots of the War of Independence were fired at Soloheadbeg in January 1919, the Volunteers around Burncourt were ready for action. The local companies in the Burncourt area were led by John Casey, Boolakennedy, and J.J. Kearney, Coolagarranroe. The war was waged without open conflict, using guerrilla tactics, as the Volunteers were poorly armed and the numbers of the British military forces and Royal Irish Constabulary (RIC) were large. The village itself and the people of Burncourt were frequently harassed by the military. Patrols from Cahir and Clogheen regularly passed through the village and squads of troops patrolled the area. This led to the formation of the flying column in Burncourt and, similar to the columns in other areas, it used hit-and-run tactics, sheltering in safe houses as the need arose.

Much of the population at the turn of the nineteenth century spoke both Irish and English, and many of the words in common usage are derived from that bilingual heritage. The townland and place names also reflect an older tradition and give an insight into the landscape and past events.

Electricity came to the valley in 1957 and was life-changing. Cooking and washing were no longer dependant on heating water over open fires. At the turn of the Millennium, in 2000, a stone was erected in the church grounds which records in perpetuity all those who lived in the parish at that time.

2

The Landscape

BURNCOURT lies on the foothills of the Galtee Mountains (Fig. 1). The Irish name for the Galtees, 'Sliabh na gCoillteach', translates as 'Mountain of the Woods', reflecting the tree cover over the lower slopes. The rock formations of the Galtee Mountains were formed when the earth's crust folded 500 million years ago, causing the Old Red Sandstone to protrude through its covering of Carboniferous Limestone and Silurian rocks to protrude, in turn, through the Old Red Sandstone. Galteemore, also known as 'Dawson's Table',[1] is the highest peak. The entire area was glaciated and the lakes in the Galtee Mountains, similar to Bay Lough in the Knockmealdown Mountains, are corrie lakes formed as the ice sheets melted and retreated about 70,000 years ago. The largest of these lakes is Lough Muskry and, to the east, a slightly smaller lake named Botheen Lough,

FIG. 1–GALTEE MOUNTAINS.

with smaller unnamed lakes across the mountain slopes. An outcrop of shattered rock overlooking the valley where Burncourt lies is known as 'O'Loughnan's Castle' (Caisleán Uí Lachnain) and, although a natural feature, has the appearance of a built structure. There is a tradition which associates O'Loughnan's Castle with a highwayman similar to Brennan on the Moor[2] of the Kilworth Mountains. Two main rivers flow southwards from the Galtees: the Shanbally river is on the west side and the Burncourt river is to the east.

The political landscape of the area can be traced through time, whereby different tribal groups controlled the region. Historical details before the arrival of Christianity, and with it literacy and written records, are obscure. Burncourt is within the ancient territory of the Déisi, who extended their control, in the centuries around the birth of Christ, into South Tipperary and as far north as east Limerick. The Déisi were superseded by the Eóganachta Cashel, who reigned until the early years of AD 900. The Eóganachta were overtaken, in turn, by the Dál Cais, who were descendants of the original Déisi and whose most famous king was Brian Boru. The Anglo-Norman invasion and subsequent colonisation saw much of the territory granted to the great lords of Ormond (the Butlers) and Desmond (the Fitzgeralds) with Anglo-Norman families such as Butler, English, Fitzgerald, Keating, Prendergast, Tobin and Walsh, amongst others, representing the tenants of the great Anglo-Norman lords. The Everards, who were initially resident in Ballyboy Castle, were granted the title of Baron, moved to Burncourt Castle in 1641, and were considered to be of Old English stock. They were originally descended from the Anglo-Normans but, as the old adage goes, they became more Irish than the Irish themselves. Ultimately the lands around Burncourt came under the ownership of Cornelius O'Callaghan. His descendant, also Cornelius O'Callaghan, Viscount Lismore, left Shanbally Castle and estate to his cousins Lady Beatrice Pole-Carew and Lady Constance Butler, daughters of the Marquis of Ormond. The castle was sold and eventually demolished. The property was divided by the Land Commission, spreading possession of the estate landscape out to individual landowners.

Mitchelstown Caves
The caves are the most extensive caverns in Ireland and lie in the Carboniferous Limestone rocks. There are two cave networks. The 'Old Cave' was known for hundreds of years and was where the Sugán Earl, James (FitzThomas) of Desmond, was taken prisoner by the White Knight of Kerry after the Geraldine revolt (1598–1601) in Munster. The rebellion was led by the Sugán Earl and his clansmen with the aim of restoring the earldom of Desmond but was quashed by Sir George Carew, who landed in Waterford in April 1600. The 'New Cave'

was discovered by Michael Condon in 1833 when he was quarrying limestone. Part of the Kingston estate which was centred in Mitchelstown, extended to Burncourt and the name 'Mitchelstown Caves' was given to newly-discovered cave. Once the caves were discovered, the Kingstons brought visitors to see the underground wonder and the names 'House of Lords', 'House of Commons', 'Cathedral' and 'Organ' were given at that time to various caverns and features.

Burncourt village
The village is located in Old Shanbally (meaning 'old town') and Toorbeg (meaning 'small field for cattle') townlands. Old Shanbally includes part of the east side of the modern village and extends southwards to Ballysheehan church. Burncourt village derives its name from the castle or the 'Burnt Court'. The lands around Burncourt and the creation of the manor of Everard's Castle is recorded in a grant to Sir Richard Everard in 1639 by Charles I, whereby 'Cloghine [Clogheen] alias Everard's Castle' was listed as well as 'Cloghine [Clogheen] or Everard's Market'. Clogheen was the original name, which became Everard's Castle and is now called Burn(t)court Castle. The manor of Everard's Castle included the castle, the lands of Ballyboy and Shanrahan and the market at Clogheen. Sir Richard and his family were in Ballyboy in 1639 and Everard's Castle was under construction. It is probable that a small hamlet existed in the Burncourt area in the seventeenth century, as indicated by the name 'Shanbally' (Seana Bhaile) or 'old village'.

1843 Ordnance Survey record
The present village was in existence at the time of the first Ordnance Survey of 1843 and this map shows the school house (now the community centre) and five

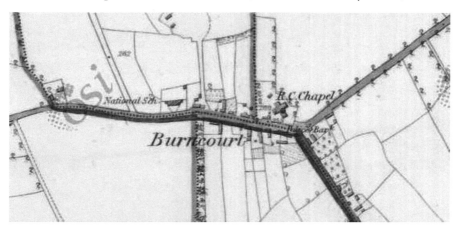

FIG. 2–EXTRACT FROM 1843 ORDNANCE SURVEY MAP.

FIG. 3–BURNCOURT VILLAGE, 2002. *COURTESY JIMMY FITZGERALD*

buildings along the north side of the street (Fig. 2). Of these, Creed's shop, Ryan's bar and Moran's house are still in existence, and one was Mary Walsh's house (now part of Hillview) while the other house was on the street where the four street-fronting houses of Hillview estate are now located (Fig. 3). The old church is also shown as a cruciform-plan building. The south side of the street had eight buildings and of these only Connolly's house, the Old Shanbally Bar and Margaret Cleary's house remain. The Old Shanbally Bar was formerly an RIC barracks. There was also a building directly opposite the present school.

Bassett's Directory of 1889
Bassett's Directory described Burncourt village as having eighteen houses. The following gives a list of occupants and businesses:

Grocers: Mrs Ml. Donohue; Jerh. Fox; Mrs M. Galvin; Thomas Geary; Ms B. Lonergan.
Post Mistress: Kate Carmen.
School, N. L: Ml. Duggan, Mrs C. Duggan.
Spirit Retailers: Ms K. Galvin; Thomas Geary.
Farmers and Residents:

Butler, James Ballyshurue	Casey, John Glengara
Casey, Ms Ballyrue	Cashin, Denis Burncourt Castle
Conway, Mrs Toormore	Corbett, John Burncourt

Dunlay, Patrick Toorbeg

English, James Toormore

Fox, Edward, Kilavinogue

Mulcahy, Mrs Ballysheehan

Ryan, John Shanbally

Priests [based in Clogheen]:

Rev. F. Meany,

Adm.; Rev. P. Coffey, CC;

Church of Ireland:

Rev. W. H. Oswald, Rector;

English, Daniel Coolantallagh

Fogarty, William Inchnamuck

McGrath, Denis Coolantallagh

Riordan, Mrs Ballyshurue

Sullivan, David Toormore

PP; Rev. T. McGrath,

Rev. W. Quealy, CC.

Rev. Arthur Graham, Curate.

Census 1911

The Census of 1911 recorded the following families in the village:

Alice and Thomas Fox, Blacksmith. Both spoke Irish and English.

Kate and John Corbett, Farmers. Four children aged 12–17. Spoke English only. Daniel Donoghue, a workman on the farm is also listed in the household.

Michael and Bridget Cashin [mother and son] Farmer Burncourt Castle. Both spoke Irish and English. Two female servants, Alice and Hannah Moloney worked in the household.

Patrick Cullinan [widower], Farmer. Spoke Irish and English.

Catherine and Michael O'Donnell, Carpenter and his wife. Spoke English only.

Anne and Kate Carmen, Dressmakers. Both spoke Irish and English.

William Luddy (Senior), his son William and daughter-in-law Mary and their three children, Hanorah, John and Thomas. William Senior was a farmer and his son was a labourer. William Senior spoke Irish and English while his son only spoke English.

Edmond and Bridget Casey, Farmers. Six children, Bridget, Patrick, Edmond, William, Ellen and Hanorah aged 12–26. Spoke Irish and English.

Garret Lonergan, Michael O'Neill and Edmond Nolan. Farm labourers. Spoke English only.

The east side of the village is in Shanbally townland and the following are listed there:

Johanna Dobbins, Seamstress. Spoke Irish and English.

Edmond and Catherine Osbourne, Farm labourer. Six children, Hannah, Bridget, John, Catherine, Margaret and oddly enough a second Hannah, aged 2–13. Spoke English only.

Daniel and Kate Dowling. Kate is listed as a dressmaker and Daniel as a tool maker. Three children, Timothy, Mary and Patrick aged 4–9. Spoke Irish and English.

Henry and Catherine Colclough, Coakley's Cross, Farmers. A farm-worker, Michael Ryan is also listed. Spoke English only.

John and Catherine Ryan, Farmers. Both spoke English and Irish. Daughter Hannah. Two domestic servants Catherine Casey and Kate O'Neill.

John, James, Eliza and Catne Riordan [brothers and sisters], Farmers. Spoke Irish and English.

Pat and Mary Maher, Farm labourer and wife. Spoke Irish and English.

Patrick and Ellen Norris, Farm labourer and wife. Two children James and Mary, an infant and year-old. Spoke English only.

Cornelius (B) Ryan, wife Catherine and daughter May, Shopkeepers. Bridie McGrath, a barmaid and four servants, Catherine Sullivan, Eliza O'Donnell, Patrick McGrath and John Meaney and a nurse Catherine Hickey were also listed in the household. All spoke English only.

John and Mary Donoghue, his mother Margaret, sister Mary and niece Bridget. A farm-worker Daniel Donovan was also listed in the household. All spoke English only.

Owen Aherne, Michael Hickey and Robert Walsh, Farm-workers. Owen Aherne spoke Irish and English and the other two only English.

John and Alice Nolan, Farm-worker and his wife. Both spoke Irish and English. Four children, Ned, Lizzie, Bridger and Mary, aged 15–27 who spoke English only.

The 1911 Census (www.census.nationalarchives.ie) shows the beautiful copperplate writing of the household heads who signed the original census forms. Irish was spoken by most.

3

Early History

TIIE EARLIEST inhabitants of the Burncourt area are unknown as there are no physical remains or historical information to show who lived in the area in antiquity. The area was possibly heavily wooded in prehistoric times but also accessible to prehistoric peoples via the river network of the Tar and Burncourt rivers, tributaries of the Suir river. Road and gas pipeline schemes in the valley between the Galtee and Knockmealdown mountain rangess have uncovered remains of prehistoric settlements which lay buried below the soil and were only uncovered when the soil was stripped. The finds included Stone Age (4000–2500 BC) and Bronze Age (2500–600 BC) houses and burial sites. In the wider area there are traces of ancient sites such as the megalithic tomb at Lissava, near Cahir, and a burial cairn at Garryroan, near Ballylooby. Ancient cooking sites, known as *fulachtaí fia*, are, in folklore, associated with the Fianna, a mythical band of warriors who, under the leadership of Fionn Mac Cumhaill, roamed the countryside. These sites are considered to be locations where communal feasting took place. *Fulachtaí fia* were uncovered at Brackbaun when the M8 was under construction, and are dated to around 1634–1454 BC and 789–425 BC. The roadworks also uncovered a corn-drying kiln in Brackbawn which was used to dry corn prior to threshing and dated to about AD 500.

The myths and legends of Burncourt also point to past peoples in the area. The townland of Glengarra and Glengarra Wood are linked to the Fianna. One of the Fianna warriors was Morna, who is said to have been the father of Gara from which Glengarra ('Glen Gara') takes its name. Gara is recorded in the Ordnance Survey letters (1840) as Gara of the Black Knee, the son of Morna. The name 'Seefin' or 'Suidhe Finn' ('Finn's Sitting Place') on the Galtee Mountains also connects the Burncourt area with the legendary Fianna.

Early Christianity
The earliest known history of the Burncourt area dates to the period AD 400–900 and is evident in the field monuments. The beginning of this period is marked by the conversion to Christianity. The Burncourt area was part of the Déisi territory, which extended from Waterford to east Limerick. The Déisi tribe also colonised parts of Wales and came in contact with Christianity; history confirms that some Christians were in Ireland before the arrival of St Patrick in the north of the country in AD 432. St Declan, known as the apostle of the Decies, is associated with Tubbrid church and St Declan's Way, which was an ancient route between Cashel and Ardmore. Tradition has it that St Declan was one of the royal dynasty of the Déisi and was instrumental in bringing Christianity to Munster in the early conversion period. He was probably preaching Christianity in the south of Ireland at the same time as St Patrick preached in the north. Early church sites are usually recognised in the landscape by circular enclosures, some physical remains of a church, cross-inscribed slabs, proximity to a holy well, proximity to bullaun stones,[3] or are evidenced in the place name or townland name. There is some indication that churches were located on the edge of ancient tribal boundaries and these are what are now parish boundaries. The organisation of the early church in Ireland was based on a federation of monasteries under the control of an abbot or bishop who claimed lineage from a founder. Apart from early monastic sites, some churches probably fulfilled a pastoral role, and private churches were also built for the use of individual families.

Early churches were probably built mainly of timber and later replaced, from about AD 900, by mortared stone buildings. The Irish word *dairthech*(oak house) was used to describe timber churches, and as these do not survive above ground, the foundations can only be discovered and dated through archaeological excavation. Similarly, churches constructed from other perishable materials such as wattle or turves (sods) leave little or no above-ground traces.

Sites of early Christian churches in Burncourt
The evidence for early Christianity around Burncourt is in the place names and the sites of holy wells. The Ordnance Survey maps and Canon Power's *The Place-Names of Decies* (published in 1907) record a church in the quarry just north of Burncourt village. The place name, 'Mullach na Cille', translates as 'Ancient Church Summit'. Canon Power records that most of the church site was cut away in the process of quarrying limestone for burning in a nearby kiln. The townland Killavenoge (Cill a'Bhionóg), on the western boundary of the parish, had the site of an ancient church (now levelled). Canon Power describes the location as

FIG. 4–EASTER WELL (TOBAR NA CÁRCA), SCART TOWNLAND.

being close to the only farm house in the townland. In the Ordnance Survey records of 1840, John O'Donovan suggested the name 'Bionóg' could be translated as 'Winoc's Church'. Winnocus was a Breton and the Feast of St Winnocus is traditionally on 5 November. The name may also stem from Unniue whose feast is on 29 August, and who, in the saints' lives, was bishop of Inis-Cathaig. The name 'Unniue' may be a corruption of 'Uninnoc' or 'Vindoc'.

The church in Ballysheehan was originally known by the ancient name of Kilmolash. The first part of the word is an Anglicisation of the Irish word 'cill', meaning 'church', and the second part refers to the saint associated with the church. The saint is probably Laishrén (or Laishrán); he is known from historical accounts of the saints and associated with the early church in Ireland. The name 'Kilmolash' therefore translates as the 'church of Laishrén' and the association with Laishrén dates the original church foundation to as early as AD 600–700. The graveyard is surrounded by a sub-circular enclosure and this is typical for churches of the early Christian period (AD 500–900) The first church at

FIG. 5–EARLY STONE CROSS AT THE EASTER WELL (TOBAR NA CÁRCA), SCART TOWNLAND.

Ballysheehan was probably constructed using wood and later replaced with a stone church. It may be that the foundations of the early church exist on the site, but these are now buried below the ground surface.

Further afield, there was the site of an ancient church in Kilcoran (Cill Chuaráin). The saint associated with the church was Cuaran. Cuaran was recorded in the Martyrology of Donegal as 'Cuaran the Wise' whose feast day is 9 February. The church site was close to a holy well which is now dried up. Similar to the church at Killavenoge, the church in Kilcoran was on the boundary of the ancient parish of Tubbrid. Fragmentary walls of a church in Rehill townland date to AD 1350–1450, but an earlier church probably stood on the site. The name of the church is Cill an Lubhair, the '*cill*' itself is indicative of an early church. The townland of Kilroe ('Cill Ghainimhe', meaning 'Church of the Sand') also takes its name from an ancient church and is so called because of its proximity to a sand-pit.

Holy wells

There is a holy well known as the 'Easter Well' (Tobar na Cárca) in Scart townland (Fig. 4) which is sometimes called 'Tobar Mullaigh Chéarta' ('The Well of the Mount of Suffering', i.e. Calvary). The well was in regular use in the early 1900s when Canon Power compiled *The Place-Names of Decies*. There is also a stone cross at the well site which may be ancient (Fig. 5). A well in Tubbrid known as 'St Kieran's Well' (Tiobraid Chiarán) goes back to the fifth century according to the *Life of St Declan*. St Declan baptised the infant Ciaran at the well. Ciaran founded the monastery at Tubbrid and was elevated to sainthood in early Christian times.

Early settlement sites

Settlement in the early Christian period was usually within ringforts. Ringforts can be considered as enclosed farmsteads of strong farmers, affording the inhabitants some protection as well as status. Ringforts are the most widespread archaeological field monuments in Ireland. They are usually known by the names '*rath*' or '*lios*' and are circular or sub-circular areas enclosed by single or multiple earthen banks formed of material thrown up from an external concentric fosse (ditch). Variations on the enclosing element include stone-faced banks or stone walls (*caher*). Although comparatively few ringforts have been excavated, it is accepted that they have a long period of use, mainly from about AD 500–900. Few historical details survive on these sites. There are ringforts in the vicinity of Burncourt village in the townlands of Ballyhurrow, Rehill and Garrandillon. Garrandillon ringfort is located on Shanbally estate and is known as 'Piper's Fort'. The townland name 'Raheen' also suggests a ringfort or 'rath', and Canon Power records that a large motte-like rath still existed at the turn of the twentieth century. The name 'Cahergal' (Cathair Gheal) in Coolagarranroe townland is translated as 'White Stones Fort' and suggests the site of a stone-fort in the area.

4

Ballysheehan Church and Graveyard

History

The church and graveyard now known as Ballysheehan are located in the townland of Old Shanbally. The ruined church in Ballysheehan is medieval in date and, on the basis of shape and form of the windows, appears to date to about AD 1400. The present church ruin was on the site of an earlier church dating to AD 600–700, originally known by the ancient name of Kilmolash and associated with St Laishrén (or Laishrán). The church is surrounded by a sub-circular enclosure, typical for churches of the early Christian period (AD 500–900). As most early churches were constructed using wood, nothing now survives above ground of the early church.

In Ireland the early church was originally based on a monastic system and controlled by abbots. In order to bring the church into line with Rome, a diocesan system was introduced in the early 1100s and bishops henceforth controlled church matters. Once the main dioceses were established, a parish system followed in the thirteenth century. The parish lands were almost inevitably based on ancient Irish family groups or clans, or in areas where the Normans had settled on the land granted to the Norman lords. In both Norman and Irish areas, laymen played an important role in the establishment and maintenance of parishes, and were benefactors of the parish churches. The right of advowson, or the right to choose a priest, was a privilege of the landlord or chief. The choice of priests was subject to the bishop's approval and this practice remained in place for centuries.

The area around Burncourt and the parish of Shanrahan belongs to the ancient territory of the Decies. This territory is approximately the same as the present Diocese of Waterford and Lismore. There are almost one hundred old churches in the diocese and, of these, almost eighty are medieval parish churches. The medieval parish churches are simple buildings, rectangular in plan, gable-ended and usually about 30–80ft (9–24.4m) in length and 22–30ft (6.7–9m) wide. The churches are aligned east–west, with the altar on the east side and a large window set in the east gable. The orientation of the church was designed to make the most of the morning light for Mass. A small window may be set into the south wall, near the altar, to provide extra light. An alcove is frequently located in the east gable, to the right of the altar. The door is usually on the west end of the church. Traces of a wooden gallery may survive on the west end of the building and this gallery would have been used as the priest's quarters or lodgings.

Ballysheehan church

The features in Ballysheehan church are typical of the Decies churches. The church is 70ft (21m) long by 28ft (8.5m) wide, which is on the larger end of the scale of church size (Fig. 6). Ballysheehan has east and west windows and a small window in the south wall. There are, unusually, two doors in Ballysheehan, both on the west side and diametrically opposed, set in the north (Fig. 7) and south

FIG. 6–BALLYSHEEHAN CHURCH AND GRAVEYARD.

FIG. 7–BALLYSHEEHAN CHURCH DOORWAY IN NORTH WALL.

FIG.8–BALLYSHEEHAN WEST WINDOW.

Fig. 9–Ballysheehan church piscina.

walls. There is some evidence that a loft existed in the west end; recesses in the west end walls may have housed structural beams that supported a wooden loft which acted as the living quarters for the priest.

Both the west (Fig. 8) and east windows are ogee-headed – an 'S'-shape-pointed head – and the window surrounds, or hood mouldings, are square. The west and east window have trefoil decoration on either side of the top of the window, below the moulding. The west window is a single light and the east window is two-light with an intermediary mullion. The window on the south wall, near the altar, has a simple rounded arch and splayed interior.

One extra surviving feature in Ballysheehan is a 'piscina', which is on the right-hand side of the east end (Fig. 9). A piscina is a basin, usually on the south side of the altar, into which the water used for washing the sacred vessels was poured. The example in Ballysheehan has carved lines radiating from a central hole. The water was poured into this hole and seeped into the ground.

The graveyard
The graveyard in Ballysheehan has over two hundred grave markers and these were detailed in a catalogue (Cleary, 2001). The graves are located mainly on the south side of the church but also extend along the east and west sides. There are

FIG. 10 (LEFT)–BALLYSHEEHAN GRAVEYARD, CELTIC CROSS MEMORIAL STONE.
FIG. 11 (RIGHT)–BALLYSHEEHAN GRAVEYARD, CELTIC CROSS MEMORIAL STONE WITH CRUCIFIXION SCENE.

no graves on the north side of the church, and this absence of graves is due to the association, in the medieval period, of the north side with paganism. The north side of churches was reserved for the excommunicated or criminals.

Some of the memorials are 'Celtic crosses', which are a nineteenth-century revival of earlier Celtic art (Fig. 10–11). The crosses are ringed and have ornate interlaced ornaments. There is one grave, which is classified as a 'Table Tomb', where the grave is under a flat memorial slab raised on four slabs, and the overall effect is of a large stone table (Fig. 12). This memorial is for Edmond O'Gorman and the first date is 1832. A single obelisk memorial marker in the graveyard marks the grave of the McGrath family (Fig. 13).

There may be many burials in the graveyard where no marker survives. The

FIG. 12–BALLYSHEEHAN
GRAVEYARD, TABLE TOMB.

FIG. 13–BALLYSHEEHAN
GRAVEYARD, OBELISK
GRAVE MEMORIAL.

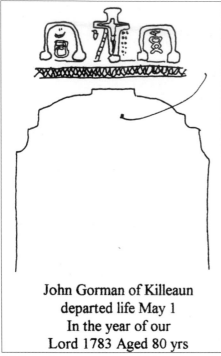

John Gorman of Killeaun
departed life May 1
In the year of our
Lord 1783 Aged 80 yrs

Erec[d] by John Nash in Mem[y], of
his son Joh[n] Nash of Bawnard
who died Jan[y] 8th 1813 Aged 39 [yrs]
who lived beloved of died lamented

FIG. 14–BALLYSHEEHAN GRAVEYARD, INSCRIPTION JOHN GORMAN, WITH CRUCIFIXION SCENE.

FIG. 15–BALLYSHEEHAN GRAVEYARD, INSCRIPTION JOHN NASH (1813), WITH CRUCIFIXION SCENE AND DOVES.

grave slabs date from the early 1700s up to the recent past. The earliest memorial is No 86 for Morgan O'Brion (O'Brien) and the first date on this is 1723. Other early stones are No 87 (Roger Flynn, 1734) and No 89 (Maurice Foley, 1740). There are a number of gravestones for the period 1760–1790. Most of the memorials are, however, for the period 1800–1890. The family names on the memorials still survive today in Burncourt.

The inscriptions

Some of the inscriptions are difficult to read and some of the spellings of both personal names and townlands may be slightly different to the modern spelling. Many of the gravestones have carved symbols, which are Passion symbols, as described in the Gospels. These include the figure of the crucified Christ, which is usually in the centre of the memorial (Fig. 14–15). The letters 'INRI' also occur, and this means 'Jesus of Nazareth, King of the Jews'. Other symbols are birds: a dove with a branch in its mouth probably represents the Resurrection; a cock crowing can represent Peter's denial of Jesus. The instruments of the Passion, including a ladder, hatchet, pincers, crown of thorns, nails and scourges, are also shown on some memorials. The use of these symbols on the memorials is undoubtedly related to popular devotion and religious belief in the salvation of the soul through the Passion and death of Christ.

Two inscriptions are particularly sad and yet hopeful. They are as follows:

Ah cruel death that could not be denied
Thou broke our bands that had so long been tied
But we will meet again on another shore
Where death himself can't break our bands no more

Farewell dear
dead but sleeping here

5

The Anglo-Normans
and the Capture of the Súgan Earl in the Caves

THE ANGLO-NORMAN invasion of Ireland in 1169 began a process which was to change the political and social fabric of Ireland. The invading army made piecemeal progress across the country, forging alliances with Gaelic chiefs and defeating others. The goal was land and, with it, wealth. For the first ten years there was a period of consolidation of territorial gains. The lands between the Galtee and Knockmealdown mountain ranges were the subject of grants to the Anglo-Norman families, and of these the Butlers (Ormond) on the east side and the Fitzgibbons (Desmond) to the west emerged as the dominant Anglo-Norman lords. Other Anglo-Norman families included the Prendergast and Keating as well as the Everard family. Everards appeared in Ireland soon after the Anglo-Norman invasion and, by the 1300s, a branch of the Everards was recorded around Fethard with a junior line in Co. Waterford.

After the invasion in 1169, and once the more active Gaelic resistance was crushed, the Anglo-Normans built castles to secure their Irish properties. Early Anglo-Norman castle-building in Munster was a deliberate and slow process, and Anglo-Norman fortresses spread to all districts, guarding passes, routes, rivers and fords. These early castles were earth-and-timber fortresses rather than stone, and are known as 'motte-and-baileys'; one of these survives in Ardfinnan, while a second large motte remains in Knockgraffon. These early Anglo-Norman fortifications appear to have continued in use for 100–150 years after they were first built. Thereafter, stone castles were constructed; examples of these early castles survive in Castlegrace while fragments of another remain in Shanrahan graveyard.

Capture of the Súgan Earl in the caves

James of Desmond was the nephew of Gerald Fitzgerald, 14th Earl of Desmond; Gerald's defeat after the rebellion of 1579–83 saw all Desmond lands confiscated and planted by Elizabethan settlers. James of Desmond, known as 'The Súgán Earl', joined forces, in 1598, with Hugh O'Neill, who was at the time waging the Nine Years War (1593–1603) against English rule in Ireland. The rebellion in Munster was quashed by Sir George Carew, who landed in Waterford in April 1600. The Súgán Earl had to go into hiding; Carew tried to hunt him down but was unsuccessful until he made contact with Edmund Fitzgibbon. Fitzgibbon, known as the 'White Knight', had lands in the Mitchelstown and Fermoy areas, as well as Shanrahan and Clogheen. The White Knight was accused by Crown forces of hiding the Súgan Earl of Desmond. In response to this accusation, and also for a reward of £1,000, the White Knight betrayed the Súgán Earl to Carew. The Súgan Earl was hiding in the caves known as 'Uaimh na Caorach Glaise' ('Cave of the Green Sheep'), and he was captured there in 1601. This cave is part of the cave system adjacent to the Mitchelstown Caves. The White Knight received his reward but was thereafter known as the man who betrayed the Earl.

6

Burncourt Castle

THE EVERARD CASTLE in Burncourt had a relatively short life. The building was completed in 1641 and was burnt in 1650, never to be reoccupied again. An old rhyme says that:

> It was seven years in building,
> Seven years living in it,
> And fifteen days it was burning.

The castle is a fortified house, constructed in the years immediately before 1641 by Sir Richard Everard and occupied from 1641–1650 (Fig. 16). A date stone of 1641 for the castle is incorporated in a wall to the south-west of the castle, in the nearby farmyard. The castle was originally called 'Clogheen' and became known as 'Burncourt' only after it was burnt in 1650.

Everard family

The family history of the Everards was published by Richard Everard in *The Irish Genealogist* in 1988–89. The Everard family appeared in Ireland soon after the Anglo-Norman invasion, and a Martin Everard is mentioned as a companion of Prince John when he went to Ireland in 1185 (Everard, 1988). Ecclesiastical taxation records of 1302–06 confirm the Everard family in the Cashel diocese. By the early fourteenth century, one branch of the Everards developed in Co. Meath, with their seat in Randlestown, and the second branch was concentrated in Co. Tipperary, principally around Fethard, with a junior line in Co. Waterford. The Everard name appears in several legal documents, including deeds and court records, and by 1585 a Redmond Everard, with James Butler, represented Co. Tipperary in parliament. John Everard, son of Redmond, was an accomplished lawyer and was appointed by Queen Elizabeth I as Second Justice of the Queen's

FIG. 16- BURNCOURT CASTLE.

Bench in 1602; the post was re-granted to John Everard by King James I in 1603. He was knighted in 1605. Of the seven judges on the Second Justice of the Queen's Bench, Sir John Everard was the only Catholic, and he was forced to resign in 1607 because he continued to refuse to take the Oath of Supremacy. He was elected to James I's Irish parliament in 1613, where he acted as leader of the Catholic opposition in a Protestant-dominated assembly.

Sir Richard Everard was the second son of Sir John and was created a baronet in 1622 by James I. Sir Richard, on his marriage to Catherine Plunkett, had been given lands in counties Cork, Limerick and Tipperary in 1620 by Sir John; his residence was Ballyboy, just east of Clogheen village. After Catherine Plunkett's death, Sir Richard married Catherine Tobin and his father again granted him the lands in 1624. The second deed mentions specifically Ballyboy, Cloghyne (Clogheen) and Kilballyboy. Sir Richard received a grant from Charles I in 1639, creating the manor of Everard's Castle, comprising the manor, castle, town and lands of Ballyboy, and the manor, castle, town and lands of Shanrahan parish, including Everard's Castle and Everard's Market. Everard's Castle was originally known as Clogheen and is now called Burncourt Castle; Everard's Market is now the town of Clogheen. Sir Richard and his family were still in Ballyboy in 1639 when Everard's Castle was under construction. The new castle was financed by the sale of lands in Cork and Limerick in the early 1630s. The Everards moved to the newly constructed castle in 1641. The Civil Survey of 1641 shows that Richard Everard's estates totalled 8,471 plantation acres, or 13,926 statute acres.

Richard Everard was Old English – as was Catherine Tobin's family, and her father had huge land tracts towards the east of the county. Both families were Catholic and Royalist. William Smyth (2006) describes Richard Everard as a modernising landowner; he brought new tenants to his estates and developed new settlements. The construction of the mansion house at Burncourt reflected Everard's wealth and status as well as Richard Everard's extensive connections at home and abroad as a parliamentarian. Sir Richard joined the Catholic Confederates in 1642 and partook in the Kilkenny parliament.

Under the Cromwellian confiscation, lands in South Tipperary were reserved for Adventurers, who were a group of English merchants, most of them from London, that had advanced money for the Cromwellian campaigns in Ireland. The Everard estate was claimed by Thomas Cunningham and Captain Lewis Dick, but was restored to Sir Redmond Everard, son of Sir Richard, in 1673 by Charles II. Sir Redmond had previously inherited the Everard land around Fethard from his cousin Nicholas, who died without issue; it seems probable that his seat was in Fethard rather than in the south of the county, in the Clogheen area.

The subsequent ownership of the lands in Clogheen is unclear. The lands around the Everard holding in Burncourt ultimately came into the ownership of Cornelius O'Callaghan, Viscount of Lismore. Sir Redmond Everard's grandson, also Sir Redmond, was orphaned at a young age and was reared by Mary Butler, Duchess of Devonshire, who owned Lismore estate. Sir Redmond had continuous financial problems and some of his lands, including Burncourt and Clogheen, were sold in 1721. One of his main creditors was Cornelius O'Callaghan, who probably acquired the land for £11,500 in settlement of the debt.

The mansion house at Burncourt was never restored and it appears that Lady Everard returned to her original home in Ballyboy. A survey of Sir Richard Everard's estate, established by the Court of Survey during a session in Clonmel on 21 February 1754, records that in the townland of Ballyboy there was 'a castle covered with thatch without repair and a thatch house likewise without repair within a bawn, lately rebuilt by the Lady Everard and some cabbins' (Everard,

1989, 538). The Court of Survey also records that 'upon the lands stands Sir Richard Everard's Mansion House, called Everards Castle the walls onely standinge and some cabins within a bawne, the sd house beinge burned is yet without repaire' (*ibid.*).

1641 rebellion

The 1641 rebellion began as an attempt by the landowners, dispossessed due to the Elizabethan plantations, to recover lands, and evolved into an alliance or confederation of Catholics, including Gaelic and 'Old English', who determined to defend their religion, their rights and their property. The revolt cost thousands of lives and was finally suppressed by the arrival of Oliver Cromwell.

Richard Everard's move to Burncourt coincided with the 1641 rebellion and he needed to protect the English tenants on his estate against attacks from the Irish rebels. Power writes in his *History of South Tipperary* (1989) that Richard Everard was regarded as an English settler at the beginning of the 1641 rebellion and had thirty-three stud mares and two thousand sheep stolen from him, but he also joined the rebellion. Everard had thirty tenant families and he moved eighty-eight people to the safety of his castle until the middle of June 1642. He was then able to bring them to the English garrison at Mitchelstown. Richard Everard joined the Catholic Confederates at the Kilkenny assembly in 1642 and was a member of the Supreme Council.

Luke Everard

Luke Everard was a nephew of Sir Richard Everard and was captured by Francis Boyle of Lismore when he attacked and burned Clogheen. In retaliation for Boyle's attack, Richard Butler attacked and burned Lismore and freed Luke and many of the prisoners captured by Boyle. A chalice was donated to the parish of Burncourt and Clogheen by Luke Everard when he married Eliza O'Donnell in 1638; it is now in Clogheen church.

Lord Inchiquin's taking of Burncourt Castle, 1648

Murrough O'Brien, or Lord Inchiquin, of Co. Clare advanced on Burncourt Castle in 1648. Inchiquin had fought against the Catholic Confederates during the 1641 rebellion and was Sir Richard Everard's enemy. Inchiquin had designs on lands in Tipperary and Waterford, and conducted a campaign of slaughter. Catherine, Everard's wife, was forced to leave the castle, and Inchiquin's soldiers carried off goods to the value of £200 from the castle. Catherine secured protection for herself, her children and tenants from Inchiquin, and this was reinforced by an order from the Duke of Ormond in April 1648. A truce was negotiated with Inchiquin and the Everards were granted compensation for goods seized during the conflict.

Oliver Cromwell in Burncourt, 1650

Political changes in England and the execution of Charles I saw the establishment of the Commonwealth, and Oliver Cromwell arrived in Ireland in 1649 in order to eliminate royalist support. After his conquest of the south-east, Cromwell resumed his campaign in January 1650 when he marched from Youghal to Tipperary, with the ultimate aim of reaching Kilkenny. A letter from Cromwell to the Speaker of the House of Commons in England records that he captured a castle in Kilbenny (Kilbehenny) on 31 January. He then marched to a 'stronghouse called Clogheen (Everard's Castle, now known as Burncourt) where I left a troop and some dragoons' (Everard 1989, 513). Cromwell recorded that he left a garrison at Everard's Castle in January 1650, and tradition has it that Catherine burnt the castle to prevent Cromwell from making use of it, returning to Ballyboy. Whatever the circumstances, the castle was burnt and never reoccupied. Richard continued in the resistance to the Cromwellian campaign, leading to his imprisonment after Ireton's siege of Limerick ended in 1651; although sentenced to death after Limerick fell, it appears he was imprisoned and died in 1660. Power (1907) also records that Rehill Castle was held by Ulster footmen and that it was captured, without resistance, by Cromwell, in person, on 1 February 1649.[4] Cromwell went from Burncourt to Cahir, where he took the castle without resistance, and then to Fethard, where again the town was taken without a shot being fired.

The castle

Burncourt Castle has a central block of rectangular plan, aligned north–south, with square flanking towers at each corner (Fig. 17). The masons who built the castle were very skilled; when the castle was surveyed by the Office of Public Works, the survey showed that there was only ¼in (6cm) difference between the angles from the north and south sides. The main door is on the west-facing wall and a sketch by Harold Leask in 1970 shows that this was accessed via a flight of steps (Fig. 18). A second entrance exists in the south-facing wall. Both doors are protected by gun loops, and these are also visible in the flanking towers.

The central block of the castle is three stories high, with a basement level in the north end of the central block and in the north-west and south-west towers. The castle originally had twenty-six gables and seven chimney stacks. The north-west and south-west towers have five floor levels, including the basement. The castle has a number of two- and three-mullioned windows, divided by transoms and crowned by ornamental square-ended hood mouldings. The basement level

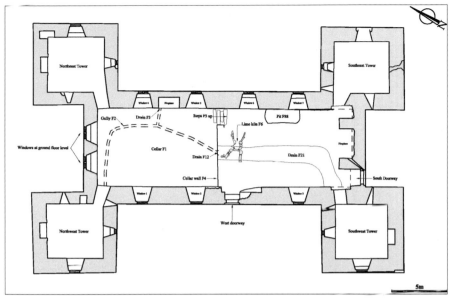

FIG. 17–PLAN OF BURNCOURT CASTLE, CENTRAL BLOCK WITH FOUR FLANKING TOWERS.

FIG. 18—BURNCOURT CASTLE, SKETCH BY HAROLD LEASK (1970).

had smaller windows than in the upper levels. The plasterwork around the windows is etched to look like brick surrounds; on the angles of the towers, the etching resembles quoin stones. Plaster survives on part of the internal walls and is best preserved in the towers. The internal partition walls were presumably of wood and the floors were carried on wall plates supported on projecting corbels.

Defensive features in the castle include the gun loops and a gallery or wooden

31

FIG. 19–BURNCOURT
CASTLE, NORTH-EAST
CORNER OF EAST FAÇADE
WITH PROJECTING CORBELS
TO SUPPORT WALL-WALK.

FIG. 20–BURNCOURT
CASTLE, 1843 ORDNANCE
SURVEY MAP WITH LINE OF
BAWN WALL (IN RED).

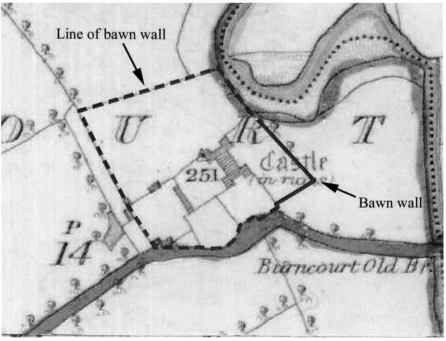

Line of bawn wall

Bawn wall

walkway along the outer side of the east and west walls of the main block; the remains of this are seen in projecting corbels, which supported the walkway (Fig. 19). Part of a bawn wall, with a corner turret, survives best along the east side, although it can be traced in the walls surrounding the castle to the north and west, and the irregular line of a boundary wall along the roadside to the south may reflect an earlier enclosing wall (Fig. 20).

Short archaeological excavations were carried out in 2003–05 in the central block to expose the cellar and lower courses of masonry, including window openings and fireplaces, and to record any other features that were uncovered. Little of the original castle occupation remained. The remarkable feature of this investigation was that there was no evidence of burning, as one would expect. Presumably when the castle was set on fire, the floors and roof collapsed inward and this should have left traces of burning in the basement and ground floor, but this was not the case. It has also been assumed that the roof was slate, but none of the slates survived and it is probable that they were salvaged for use elsewhere, given the high cost of slates and lead in the seventeenth century. The castle was abandoned after the fire and this suggests that it was considered beyond repair, either due to financial considerations, or perhaps Catherine Everard lacked the inclination to return to the castle.

The excavation exposed a cobbled cellar floor and the cellar was about 6.5ft (2m) high when in use (Figs 21–22). The cellar was presumably used to store foodstuffs, subterranean conditions providing a cool atmosphere. One of the most unusual features of the excavation was the foundation deposit uncovered under the east wall. A mature cow was killed, dismembered and placed at the foundation level of the wall (Fig. 23). Some meat was taken from the carcass before burial. This type of practice is linked to pagan tradition and, perhaps, a fertility cult rather than to the traditions of the wealthy, educated Catholic upper class of South Tipperary. The deposit may reflect the continuing survival of earlier customs, perhaps even after the rationale for the action was forgotten. Alternatively, it may be that the builders believed that the burial of a valuable animal would bring luck and prosperity to those living in the castle. Given the history of the castle, this was sadly not to be.

There were very few finds from the excavation. An unusual item was a fire-dog, or piece of fireside furniture, which was found in the cellar (Fig. 24). The decoration on the fire-dog is of a coat of arms, identified by the Chief Herald of Arms as belonging to the Earl of Shannon, a title created in the mid-eighteenth century. The fire-dog post-dated the castle burning and was probably used in the later house built beside the castle, Chearnley's house.

FIG. 21–BURNCOURT CASTLE, STEPS LEADING TO CELLAR.

FIG. 22–BURNCOURT CASTLE, COBBLED CELLAR FLOOR EXPOSED DURING 2005 ARCHAEOLOGICAL EXCAVATION.

FIG. 23–BURNCOURT CASTLE, FOUNDATION DEPOSIT OF COW PLACED PARTLY UNDER THE EAST WALL.

FIG. 24–CAST-IRON FIREDOG FOUND IN THE CELLAR OF BURNCOURT CASTLE, 2005.

FIG. 25–BURNCOURT CASTLE, SKETCH BY ANTHONY CHEARNLEY LOOKING EAST; CHEARNLEY'S HOUSE ON LEFT.

FIG. 26–BURNCOURT CASTLE, SKETCH BY ANTHONY CHEARNLEY, LOOKING WEST FROM THE RIVER.

Chearnley's house

A large house was built adjacent to the ruins of Burncourt Castle by Anthony Chearnley around 1740 (Figs 25–26). Chearnley was married to Ann Gervais and had one child, a boy called Thomas. On the death of his wife he married Janet, daughter of Richard Musgrave of Salterbridge, near Cappoquin, Co. Waterford, and had a further ten children. Chearnley appears to have moved to Salterbridge, and his descendants still lived there until the late 1860s.

Chearnley's estate was advertised for sale in the *Cork Mercantile Chronicle* newspaper on 19 July 1801. His tenants were listed as follows:

Philip O'Brien, Upper Burncourt (104 acres); Thomas Beauchamp, Lower Burncourt (11 acres); Henry Walsh and Edmond Walsh, Killavenoge (16 acres); William Casey, Cullenagh (30 acres); Philip O'Brien, Ballysheehan (45 acres); William Lonergan, Raheen (100 acres).

Other lands located outside Burncourt amounted to 357 acres, making the Chearnley estate 663 acres.

Chearnley was an architect who also sketched, and two of his sketches of the ruined Burncourt Castle survive. One sketch (Fig. 25) shows part of his house, which was two storeys with an attic. The house had a slate roof (the slates may have been salvaged from the ruins of Burncourt Castle) and projecting attic windows. The castle is shown in the background to the north, and a gateway led from Chearnley's house to a landscaped garden. The second sketch (Fig. 26) is a view of the castle from the river and shows the castle more intact than today, with several tall chimney stacks. Chearnley's house was burnt down by the Black and Tans around 1920.

7

Penal Times

A SERIES of penal laws were enacted in Ireland from around 1695, when Catholics were obliged to swear an oath of loyalty to the British monarchy and accept them as head of the church. This was contrary to Catholic beliefs. The laws were designed to humiliate Catholics and forbade them to practice their religion, to teach school, to hold any public office and to buy land. There were also laws prohibiting Catholics from leasing land for over thirty-one years, owning a horse valued over £5, and marrying a Protestant. If churches were built, they had to be of wood and away from the main thoroughfares. Under the Penal Laws, all Catholic bishops were banished from Ireland. Ordinary priests were tolerated but the absence of bishops to ordain further priests was to ensure that existing priests were not replaced. Priests had to register from 1704 onwards and give particulars about themselves.

Out of the Penal Laws developed attendance at Mass at locations outside churches and paths that led to Mass rocks, or other secretive locations; it also prompted education of Catholics in hedge schools.

Mass paths
At least two Mass paths are known in Burncourt. The memory of them remains in local tradition and none are marked as Mass paths on the Ordnance Survey maps. One path led south from the village, across Old Shanbally townland to the west of Maher's Wood (Fig. 27). A stile (Fig. 28) on the north wall of the Long Road marks the southern end of this path. A second Mass path was from Monaloughra to Rehill. This path led to a flat limestone rock, which in Penal times, may have served as an altar. Bishop John Brenan (see page 40) wrote in 1672 that there were no Mass-houses in many parts of the Diocese of Waterford and Lismore and that priests had to celebrate Mass on mountains or in open country. The old chapel (*an seana shéipéal*) in Scart is the site of a church from

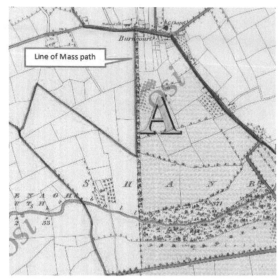

FIG. 27–LINE OF MASS PATH FROM BURNCOURT
VILLAGE TO THE LONG ROAD IN SHANBALLY
TOWNLAND.

Penal times. A place name in Carrigmore townland known as 'Lag a'tSagairt' ('The Priest's Hollow') suggests a hiding place, perhaps, for a priest on the run during Penal times. A place name in Coolagarranroe townland – 'Clair an Aifrinn' ('The Mass Trench') – is also reminiscent of a past when Mass was said in secret in the countryside. The ruined church at Tubbrid is one of the few examples of a seventeenth century church of the people, and was erected by Dr Geoffrey Keating in 1644. An inscription over the door asks for prayers for Fr Eugene O'Duffy and Dr Geoffrey Keating, and it is also the burial place of Archbishop Brenan of Cashel.

Hedge schools

As the Penal Laws forbade Catholics education, the only schooling available to the poor was through illegal hedge schools, where the pupils paid a small fee to attend. Classes were held initially in hedgerows and on byways, and later in cabins or sheds. By the turn of the nineteenth century, the hedge schools were operating openly. There were three of these types of schools recorded in the Burncourt area in the early 1800s. There are no details of who taught in the schools, and the subjects were presumably basic reading, writing and arithmetic, and possibly some Latin.

Geoffrey Keating (Seathrún Céitinn)

Geoffrey Keating (1569–1644) was born at Moorstown Castle and was the son of a well-to-do Catholic family of Old English stock. Olden (1993) identifies Keating's birthplace as Burgess, Ballylooby, where a commemorative plaque was erected in 1990. Simington (1931) lists the only large house (Burgess Mansion) in Burgess in 1640 as a thatched mansion owned by 'Hugh MaCragh of Burgess … Irish Papist', and it is unlikely Keating was born there rather than at the family home in Moorstown Castle. Keating trained for the priesthood in a Jesuit college in

FIG. 28 –STILE AT SOUTHERN END OF MASS PATH.

Bordeaux between 1603–10 and returned to Ireland to continue his Catholic ministry. He is known to have served in the parish of Outragh, about four miles from Cahir.

Geoffrey Keating is reputed to have irked the local gentry with his sermons on immorality. This happened in about 1620 when Keating spoke on the morality of Elinor Laffan, who reported him to Donough O'Brien, Earl of Thomond and President of Munster, who, in turn, offered a reward for Keating's capture, forcing him to go into hiding. One of the stories is that Keating sheltered in a cave in the woods in the Glen of Aherlow; Power (1907) cites a local narrative that Keating hid for a time in the recesses of Rehill Wood. It is more likely that sanctuary was provided by the Butlers, either in Cahir Castle or Rehill Castle.[5] Keating's major work, *A History of Ireland (Foras Feasa ar Éireann)*, was compiled at this time; he had access to the main source books, which were possibly in the Butler library in Cahir. When Donough O'Brien died in 1624, Keating returned to the old parish of Tubbrid (Ballylooby and Duhill), where he continued to minister. Keating is buried in Tubbrid.

Keating travelled extensively, copying old Irish manuscripts; *A History of Ireland* chronicled historical events, myths and legends, and was published in about 1634. It was written in Irish and later translated into English and Latin. The source material for Keating's *A History of Ireland* was earlier works on the history of Ireland, such as *Cogadh Gaedhel re Gallaibh* (*The War of the Irish with the Foreigners*) and *Leabhar Gabhala* (*The Peopling of Ireland and Reigns of Kings*), and the work was divided into two sections – one dealing with pre-Christian Ireland and the second chronicling the time from St Patrick to the coming of the Normans.

Keating also wrote *The Three Shafts of Death* (*Tri Bhíor Gaoithe an Bháis*), which was a theological work on the loss of grace and the punishment of hell. He also wrote poetry. This work helped promote a sense of national identity among the Gaelic Irish and Old English, to the detriment of new English planters who came after the Cromwellian wars.

Bishop John Brenan

Canon Power wrote an article in 1932, *A Bishop of the Penal Times*, detailing the life of Bishop John Brenan, who had links to the Burncourt area. John Brenan was born in Kilkenny around 1625 and, as his parents were well-to-do, he was educated initially in Kilkenny and ultimately in the Jesuit college in Rome, where he was ordained alongside his friend Oliver Plunkett.[6] Oliver Plunkett was appointed Archbishop of Armagh and Primate of All Ireland in 1669, returning to Ireland while John Brenan remained in Rome. John Brenan was appointed Bishop of Waterford and Lismore in 1671, and returned to Ireland. The Ireland that Bishop Brenan returned to was initially one where the Penal Laws were not vigorously imposed. The new Bishop of Waterford and Lismore had to deal, however, with the poverty of his flock and of his priests, and there was also a substantial reward for his capture. Bishop Brenan managed to elude British government officials by being given refuge and was received by the few Catholic nobility and gentry that remained in Ireland; one of his hiding places was at Rehill. Rehill, at that time, was a castle and mansion of the Butlers. Bishop Brenan wrote to the papal nuncio in 1672, stating that some English Protestant gentlemen had invited him to their houses and that these men had protected priests during times of persecution. He also wrote that, as there was no bishop in the diocese for forty years, he confirmed many people. Parishes were united by Bishop Brenan because of the scarcity of priests, and so Burncourt and Clogheen were joined, amongst others. Bishop Brenan spent a couple of months from late 1673 with his old friend Oliver Plunkett in Armagh, where both slept in a shack and had to flee from danger in January 1674 by trekking through deep snow.

Bishop Brenan was appointed Archbishop of Cashel around 1675, but remained as the administrator of Waterford and Lismore as well as being responsible for all the other dioceses in Munster. He lived somewhere around Cahir, which was on the frontier of both Cashel and Lismore. Only fifty priests were working in the combined dioceses of Waterford and Lismore and Cashel, and synods, or meetings of priests, were convened by Bishop Brenan throughout the dioceses, including one in Ardfinnan in 1677. The synods were to tighten up on discipline within the priesthood.

While Catholic persecution was less severe in the years 1676–78, it again became widespread from 1679–85. Oliver Plunkett was arrested in 1679 and sent to London for trial, where he was executed by being hanged, drawn and quartered. Archbishop Brenan chose to stay in Ireland and had to go into hiding. He ended his days in Rehill, where he died in 1693, and was buried in Tubbrid in Geoffrey Keating's tomb.

8

Troubled Times in the Eighteenth Century

The Whiteboys

Changing landholding patterns from 1730–60 saw new tenants arrive in the valley between the Galtees and Knockmealdown Mountains, which resulted in the displacement of native landholders. Smyth (1976) records that this movement was towards poorer land on the mountain slopes. Smyth notes that, apart from this, former commonage was being enclosed by landlords and this made land scarcer. Land rents increased dramatically from about 1750 and this created an even poorer peasantry: a landless class known as cottiers, who struggled to survive by labouring and growing what they could in their small plots. The backlash to this was the Whiteboy movement, beginning around 1760 and continuing into the 1770s. The Whiteboys were originally known as the 'Levellers', as they tore down fences and caused damage to landlords' property, setting fire to houses, maiming animals and destroying crops. The Whiteboys were so called because they wore white shirts over their clothes.

This was also during Penal times, when Catholics were impeded in land acquisition. There were also obligations on the Catholics to pay tithes to support the Protestant Church. The tithes were collected by the tithe proctor, who was one of the most hated officials. Pasturage was tithe-free; tillage farmers and cottiers bore the burden of tithes – particularly the cottier, who had to till ground to support his family.

Clogheen and the surrounding districts constituted one of the major centres of Whiteboy activity; the first incident was in Drumlummin townland, which was part of Lord Cahir's estate. Maurice Bric (1985) records many incidents in Shanbally, including property destruction and meetings. John Bagwell of Shanbally, who was the high sheriff for Tipperary, meted out harsh justice to Whiteboy members who were caught.

FIG. 29–FR NICHOLAS SHEEHY. *COURTESY E. O'RIORDAN, 2014*

Fr Nicholas Sheehy

Fr Nicholas Sheehy was parish priest of Shanrahan, Ballysheehan and Templetenny (Fig. 29). Ed O'Riordan published the details of Fr Sheehy's life in *The Case of Fr Nicholas Sheehy* (2014). Nicholas Sheehy was born into a well-to-do Catholic family, possibly in Barretstown, Fethard, in 1728, although T.A. Murphy (1993) suggests his birthplace was Glenaheiry, Co. Waterford, where Francis Sheehy, his father, had settled. Sheehy was sent to Louvain in Belgium to be educated; from there he entered the Irish College at Santiago de Compostelo, Spain, where he was ordained in 1750. He returned to Waterford, and from there was transferred to Newcastle in 1753. He was reassigned to the combined parishes of Shanrahan, Ballysheehan and Templetenny in 1756, areas which were centres of Whiteboy activity. His connection to the Whiteboy movement is not established but he had a sense of social justice and consideration for the plight of the poor. William Burke[7] details the cost of rents and tithes, and the condition of the cottier class from 1750 onwards; all of this must have been of concern to Fr Sheehy. Indeed, the tithe proctor in Ballyporeen required 5s. for every marriage performed by a priest, and Fr Sheehy strenuously resisted this (Murphy, 1993).

Fr Sheehy was considered by the authorities to be in league with the Whiteboys and in May 1763 he was charged with unlawful assembly, promoting insurrection and rebellion, and assaulting John Bridge at Shanbally. In February 1765 he was again charged with high treason, with a price of £300 on his head. Fr Sheehy requested that he be tried in Dublin, where he was hoping for a fair trial. Cornelius O'Callaghan of Shanbally tried to help Fr Sheehy and offered him one hundred guineas to aid his escape out of Tipperary in 1765, but Fr Sheehy declined. He was acquitted in Dublin of the charge of promoting rebellion but re-arrested on a trumped-up charge of murder and brought to Clonmel. The supposed murder victim was John Bridge, who was a Whiteboy informer and who claimed Fr Sheehy was involved in the Whiteboy movement. Other charges included the attempted murder of John Bagwell of Shanbally, and of Bagwell's brother William. At the trial in Clonmel, one of the witnesses was 'a lady of easy virtue' (a prostitute) named Mary Brady, alias Moll Dunlea, well known to the common soldiers who Fr Sheehy had denounced. She claimed that she saw Fr Sheehy strike the corpse of John Bridge and that Bridge's body was transported for burial in Ballysheehan cemetery by a group that included Fr Sheehy. Other accusers included John Toohy, a horse thief who was in jail in Kilkenny at the time and who claimed he saw Fr Sheehy strike John Bridge with a billhook which split his skull. Witnesses for the defence included Robert Keating from Knockagh, outside Cahir, who was a wealthy Catholic and who swore Fr Sheehy was in his house on the night of the supposed murder.

Fr Sheehy was convicted and on 15 March 1766 he was hanged, drawn and quartered in Clonmel. After hanging, his head was severed and stuck on a spike at Clonmel jail. The headless body was dragged through the streets of Clonmel, but received a proper burial in Shanrahan cemetery. Fr Sheehy's head remained on the spike at Clonmel jail for twenty years before his sister, Mrs Burke, was finally allowed to take it away and have it buried with his body in Shanrahan. Those that testified against Fr Sheehy died within a short time, of various causes. Mary Brady was found dead in a ditch in Kilkenny and Toohy contracted leprosy.

Others arrested around the time of Fr Sheehy's trial were Edmund Sheehy, a cousin of Fr Sheehy, James Farrel of Rehill and James Buston of Killroe, who were all well-to-do Catholics. These men were also charged with Whiteboy activity and complicity in John Bridge's murder. They were also executed and were hung in Cockpit Lane, Clogheen, in 1766.

9

Shanbally Castle and Estate

Viscount Lismore (O'Callaghan) estate

The lands around the Everard holding in Burncourt ultimately came into the ownership of Cornelius O'Callaghan of Lismore. Sir Redmond Everard's grandson, also Sir Redmond, was orphaned at a young age and was reared by Mary Butler, Duchess of Devonshire, who owned Lismore estate. Sir Redmond had continuous financial problems and some of his lands, including Burncourt and Clogheen, were sold in 1721. One of his main creditors was Cornelius O'Callaghan, who probably acquired the land in settlement of the debt.

William Smyth published a study of the O'Callaghan estate in 1976, where he documented the development from about 1730. This was a time of economic growth, as there was a demand for wool, beef, bacon and butter, and it also saw land being enclosed and marginal land being reclaimed. The O'Callaghan family were now permanently resident in Burncourt, in Old Shanbally House at Coakley's Cross.

Old Shanbally House

The location of the O'Callaghan mansion house at Coakley's Cross[8] preceded the construction of Shanbally Castle. The site is shown on the Ordnance Survey map of 1841 as 'Shanbally House' (Fig. 30). The house was built around 1735–41 by Cornelius O'Callaghan and there are now few indications of its former existence except large lime trees which remain on the northern fence side, opposite McGrath's house; local information suggests that these were the remnants of a tree-lined entrance. Any grand house had more than one entrance; there was probably also one to the south, where the wall curves inwards at the junction with the road to Clogheen. The Ordnance Survey map shows another entrance on the west side, and the grounds are depicted as landscaped with wooded areas. Other landscape features of the O'Callaghan mansion house were

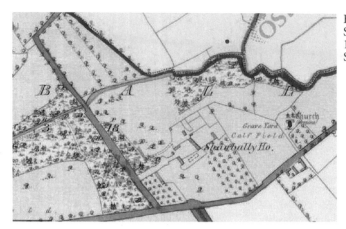

FIG. 30–OLD
SHANBALLY HOUSE,
1843 ORDNANCE
SURVEY MAP.

an artificial lake and some of the enclosing walls. William Smyth (1976) also records that the house had twenty-six chimneys and the landholdings of the O'Callaghan estate at the time were 600 acres. The house was still in existence in the early 1900s and is described by the Ordnance Survey as 'Old Shanbally House'. William Smyth (2006) notes that the account books recorded that a number of tradesmen and labourers on the estate came from Toorbeg. Cornelius O'Callaghan had three sons, Cornelius, Robert and Thomas, and of these Cornelius, who was born in 1742, became entitled in 1785 as Baron Lismore, again showing that the family were upwardly mobile and entering aristocracy. Cornelius's son, also Cornelius, became Viscount Lismore in 1806.

Tipperary landlords spent little of their incomes on improving their estates in the late eighteenth century; any improvements that took place were carried out by the tenants (Power, 1993). One notable exception was the O'Callaghans of Old Shanbally House, who sponsored land improvement such as drainage, remodelling of the landscape, the introduction on new tenants and resettlement of existing tenants. Clogheen was developed as an estate village in the 1740s when a number of houses were built to accommodate artisans and manufacturers (Power, 1993). Tenants on the estate were also encouraged to build good quality housing with a grant of £10.

Farming

The prosperity of the O'Callaghans is also evident in the amount of produce from their land and that they were granted a licence to hold three new annual fairs. Two fairs were in Ballysheehan townland, which were held on 27 August and 4 December, and other fairs were in Clogheen on 6 April, Whit Monday, 28 October and 12 December. The estate itself was one of larger farms worked by tenant farmers who had their individual farms, and smaller holdings, also held by tenants, who had mediocre resources. Cottiers, the landless class, had small plots on which to grow potatoes and were hired as labourers. Farming was mixed and mainly included cattle, dairying (including butter) and increased wheat production towards the close of the 1700s. Sheep and pigs were also kept. Wheat was sold to the mills in Clogheen and Clonmel. The estate also hired masons, carpenters and quarrymen, as well as shepherds, foresters and gardeners.

Apart from farming, the O'Callaghan estate began to create forestry. Smyth (1976) has shown that the account books of the estate included regular orders to nurseries in Clonmel, Cork, Dublin, Bristol and Scotland for thousands of Scotch fir, larch, oak and beech. Baron Cornelius O'Callaghan's brother (either Robert or Thomas), who was in the Indian army, acquired more exotic trees for the estate; cedar (*deodara*) and arboreal rhododendron were sourced in the Himalayan Mountains in India. The redwoods came from California and were presumably bought from specialist nurseries.

Prosperity and decline
Cornelius O'Callaghan, the son of the Cornelius who had built Shanbally House, prospered and was created a baron in 1785. The estate was also expanded towards the north and south to over 1,200 acres. The wealth from farming allowed for new buildings and Clogheen was expanded with a new market house, residential buildings, the street was widened and new bridges were built. The O'Callaghans also expanded their estate around Burncourt. The Ordnance Survey letters of 1839 list Viscount Lismore's holdings and included the townlands of Ballysheehan, Cullenagh, Crannagh, Carrigmore, Coolantallagh, Garrandillon, Glencallaghan, Inchnamuck, Shanbally, Scart West, Toorbeg and Toormore. Ballyhurrow, Boolakennedy, Glengarra, Monaloughra and Rehill were in the estate of Lord Glengall of Cahir and Rehill House was owned by William Fennell, Esq.

The fortunes of many estates in Ireland declined when the Napoleonic Wars ended in Europe; there was less demand for provisions from 1817–1830. This resulted in a drop in the price of produce and had a knock-on effect on estate income.

Shanbally Castle
The early years of the 1800s saw a boom in country house building and much of the work was in Gothic or Classical styles. English architects were commissioned to design new mansions, including John Nash, who designed Shanbally Castle and Mountain Lodge, as well as the Swiss Cottage, the Erasmus Smith building and St Paul's church in Cahir. A Nash-designed castle at Lough Cutra, Co.

FIG. 31–NORTH FAÇADE, SHANBALLY CASTLE.

FIG. 32–SOUTH FAÇADE, SHANBALLY CASTLE.

Galway is the same as Shanbally Castle, and is still occupied. Local architects were also employed, such as the Tinsleys from Clonmel, who designed many buildings in Cahir, including The Square. Many of the houses were only enjoyed by their builders for a short time as the Great Famine of 1846–48 was a disaster for landlords as well as tenants.

FIG. 33–NORTH FAÇADE OF SHANBALLY CASTLE WITH PROJECTING PORT-COCHÈRE.

Shanbally Castle was built by Cornelius O'Callaghan, Viscount Lismore, a descendant of the man who acquired the Everard land. The castle was completed around 1812. The castle was the largest of the Nash-designed castles in Ireland. The architectural style of Shanbally is Gothic, with rectangular and pointed windows (Figs 31–32). The entrance had a porte-cochère, a projecting porch that was large enough for wheeled vehicles to pass under (Fig. 33). Round and octagonal towers formed the corners of the main central building, and battlements and machicolations (a wall-walk at roof level) gave the appearance of a medieval castle. Internally, there was a large entrance hall with a bifurcating or branching stairway ascending to the upper rooms. The ceilings of most of the main rooms were decorated with ornate plasterwork (Fig. 34). The ground floor also had a number of reception rooms and a library while the upper floor was occupied by the bedrooms, which were accessed by a corridor with an arched ceiling.

The gardens were laid out by Humphry Repton, a famous British landscape designer. The style was an unplanned, slightly wild appearance where the garden merged into the natural surroundings of a landscape bounded by the Galtees to the north and Knockmealdowns to the south. The overall effect was picturesque, with landscaped gardens leading out onto the wider countryside. An artificial lake was created to the south by damning a stream (Fig. 35). Glasshouses were to the west and all that remains of these is a high wall.

FIG. 34–ORNAMENTAL
PLASTERWORK CEILING
OVER CENTRAL
STAIRCASE.

FIG. 35–SHANBALLY
LAKE.

FIG. 36–GATE LODGE TO SHANBALLY CASTLE.

There are some indications in the 1911 Census of the staff working on the estate. Many were Church of Ireland, although a few Catholics were also employed. Housemaids included Barbara Poole, a widow, and Henrietta Browne, both from Dublin and Sarah Gilbert, a laundress – all of them Church of Ireland. John Frazer worked as a gardener and was Presbyterian but was married to Grace, a Church of Ireland woman, and they had three children, aged 6–10, Rose, Helen and Kenneth, who were brought up as Church of Ireland. Laurence Clarke, a former RIC constable, worked on the estate and was married to Catherine; they had three children, aged 9–17. All were Roman Catholic. Michael Hickey worked on the farm. James Leech, a plumber, and Daniel Dowd, his apprentice, were Roman Catholics and originally from Dublin. William and Johanna Macken lived in the gate lodge at Glengarra Wood and were caretakers.

Viscount Lismore left the castle to his cousins Lady Beatrice Pole-Carew and Lady Constance Butler, daughters of the Marquis of Ormond. The castle was sold by Major Paddy Pole-Carew in 1954 and demolished by the Land Commission in 1960. An account of the demolition by Randall McDonnell in *The Lost Houses of Ireland* (2002) states that government civil servants ordered the roof and fittings to be removed. The battlements were hacked down despite protests from Denis Gwynn of the Arts Council and the destruction continued from September 1954 until 1960 when explosives were used in March to finally demolish the castle.

Only the gate lodges, some of the estate houses and the wall enclosing land immediately adjacent to the castle now remain. The entrance lodge to Shanbally

FIG. 37–GATE LODGE TO
MOUNTAIN LODGE AT
GLENGARRA WOOD.

FIG. 38–TEA HOUSE, SHANBALLY.

in Scart townland is an architectural gem built in 1914 (Fig. 36). The entrance to Shanbally estate beside this gate lodge was originally a broadly curved limestone wall with wrought iron railings which have now fallen into disrepair. A second entrance lodge on the west side remains in good condition and nestles beside a nicely built curved limestone wall. Glengarra Lodge (Fig. 37) was built

FIG. 39–GLENGARRA WOOD AVENUE TO MOUNTAIN LODGE, LINED WITH EXOTIC TREES.

around 1880 and is the earliest of the gate lodges. Ornate houses in Carrigmore and the farm steward's house in Shanbally also remain.

The tea house

The tea house (Fig. 38) is on the south side of the site of the former Shanbally Castle and is perched on the top of a hill overlooking Shanbally Lake. The tea house is what is known as a 'garden folly' and was used to sit out in the garden for a cup of tea, or for contemplation or writing. Some garden follies were large enough to hold banquets or served as landmarks, or may have been erected to commemorate somebody. The tea house in Shanbally is a small tower or gazebo built in the Gothic style of architecture, similar to Shanbally Castle. The tea house is two-storey, octagonal in plan and has round-headed windows with dressed stone surrounds. There is a projecting brick battlemented parapet at roof level which has elliptical arches and circular niches.

The O'Callaghan estate began to create commercial forestry in the late 1700s and planted thousands of Scotch fir, larch, oak and beech. The grove of cedar trees that stood near Mountain Lodge may have been planted as early as the early 1800s. Samuel Lewis (1837) records that Cornelius O'Callaghan, Viscount Lismore surrounded Mountain Lodge with a plantation of 150 acres. Exotic trees line the avenue from Glengarra Lodge to Mountain Lodge and include redwoods from California (Fig. 39) while the present car park in Glengarra includes a

FIG. 40–EUROPEAN SILVER FIR (*ABIES ALBA*).

redwood and silver fir (Fig. 40). Arboreal rhododendron from the Himalayan Mountains provide a magnificent display of colour in Glengarra Wood during late spring.

Mountain Lodge

The lodge is also a John Nash-designed building and was built as part of the Shanbally estate (Fig. 41). The original purpose was a shooting lodge from where shooting parties probably shot deer in the woods and grouse and pheasant in the surrounding mountainside. The original building survives intact; features include the original front door, a circular drawing room with round bay windows to the west (Fig. 42), neo-Gothic small-pane timber-sash windows, wrought iron valence to the overhanging eaves, internal joinery, panelled doors, fireplaces, decorative plasterwork, and lath and plaster ceilings. Mountain Lodge was leased to An Óige, who converted it into a youth hostel that was officially opened in 1939 (Fig. 43). The work on the building was undertaken by volunteers from An Óige (Fig. 44).

FIG. 41–MOUNTAIN LODGE.

FIG. 42–MOUNTAIN LODGE, WINDOWS IN THE ROUND ROOM.

FIG. 43–OPENING OF MOUNTAIN LODGE AS AN ÓIGE HOSTEL IN 1939. *COURTESY LEONARD GODSIL, CORK–KERRY BRANCH AN ÓIGE*

Dinner at the lodge

On 29 June, *The Limerick Reporter* newspaper gave an account of a dinner at Mountain Lodge in 1841. The dinner was held on 15 June and was described as a 'sumptuous rural dinner' hosted by Mr 'Wm. Lonergan' of Caher for his clerical friends of the dioceses of Cashel and Waterford. Eighty-six people were invited. A romantic picture of the landscape is described as 'wild and enchanting being exhibited in full relief by the dark misty light of a clouded sun ... here nature scattered her wondrous works in wild profusion ... A dinner taken at such a remarkable spot by a party of patriots and scholars.'

Those attending were called to the meal at three o'clock by a 'hoarse blast of the war trumpet from the mountains and caverns' and those attending were 'seated before a profusion of sumptuous viands [food]'. Dr Tobin, pastor of Cashel, presided over the dinner table and much of the talk was on the forthcoming general election for the British House of Commons, which was to take place from 29 June–22 July (the slow pace of communication in 1841 meant the election was over several days). Cornelius O'Callaghan, Viscount Lismore

FIG. 44–GROUP OF VOLUNTEER WORKERS AT MOUNTAIN LODGE, NOVEMBER 1939, DURING WORK TO DEVELOP YOUTH HOSTEL. *COURTESY LEONARD GODSIL, CORK-KERRY BRANCH AN ÓIGE*

was elected for Tipperary from 1835–1837, and for Waterford (Dungarvan) from 1838–1841. Richard Lalor Sheil (Bansha) was also an MP for Tipperary during this period and both Sheil and O'Callaghan were Liberals. The Conservative Party won the election in Britain in 1841.

Those attending the dinner also discussed the trial and execution of Fr Sheehy, which was described as a 'legal murder of an innocent priest'. Evictions and the diet of the poor were also topics of conversation and the 'lumper' potato was mentioned. Little did the group realise that famine was to sweep across the country in the following years. The report in the paper also noted that, apart from debate and discussion, the evening was 'enlivened by the best patriotic songs and melodies of the various countries of Europe in the French, Italian and Spanish languages'. The evening finished at about eight o'clock. Presumably many dinner parties were held at the lodge over time. Michael O'Gorman of Bawnard recounted seeing Lady Beatrice, Lady Constance and their companions driving to the lodge in pony and traps, and a supply cart for food and drink, including flagons of whiskey, was brought to the lodge.

The lodge was leased to An Óige for use as a youth hostel from the 1930s and

57

this continued until it was closed in 2012. Many of the youth hostellers or 'hikers', as they were known, came from Cork City and trips involved several good nights of singing and dancing around a bonfire.

Shanbally cricket team

The years following the Famine, particularly from the 1850s, saw the landed gentry promote cricket as a recreational amusement, and no less so on Shanbally estate. Cricket became very popular between 1873–1875, but ultimately went into decline due to the rise of the Gaelic Athletic Association, founded in 1884, and the ban on 'foreign games'. Cricket games were usually followed by fine meals held in marquees, with military bands and a ball in the evening. Other sporting activity included racing. Shanbally Cricket Club played Tramore Cricket Club on the estate in 1871 and won. *The Clonmel Chronicle* gave an account of a match on 18 June between Shanbally Cricket Club and Lismore. The Shanbally club left the field as they were hissed and booed at by the Lismore supporters.

10

Roads and Bridges

THE OLDEST ROADS in Tipperary – which were probably no more than tracks – are those associated with pilgrimages and routes linking the ancient churches. One route known as the 'Rian Bó Phádraig' ('the Track of St Patrick's Cow') goes from Cashel to Goatenbridge and over the Knockmealdown Mountains to Ardmore. The route links the ancient ecclesiastical centres of Cashel and Ardmore. There were also tracks to holy wells such as St Kieran's well in Tubbrid and the Easter Well (Tobar na Cárca) in Scart. Canon Power, in *The Place-Names of Decies*, records an ancient road ('Bóthar na Miorán' or 'Bóthar na Miorcán') in Scart townland, which ran east and west through the townland. A place name in Killavenoge townland to the west of Burncourt village is recorded by Power (1932) as Bóithrín a' Mhinirtéir ('The Minister's Little Road), which may be a Mass path used in Penal times.

Roads were constructed as part of a drive towards a better commercial network across the county. The grand juries, which were made up of well-to-do landowners nominated by the county sheriff, not only presided over court assizes (hearings and inquests); they also had charge of road repairs and construction from the early 1600s and were given statutory powers in 1739 to construct new roads. One of the earliest roads in the area was the post-road which went from Clonmel via Marlfield to Ardfinnan, Clogheen, Ballyporeen and on to Mitchelstown. This was also the road travelled by the Bianconi coaches from 1821–1853. Bianconi coaches, a horse-drawn carriage service, initially travelled around Munster, beginning in 1815 with a Clonmel–Cahir route and later expanding to all major towns in Munster and further afield; the coaches also carried the mail.

Burncourt village is surrounded by a myriad of roads and the dates in which they were made are obscure. Some roads probably existed from the time of the building of Burncourt Castle in the late 1630s or earlier, while some are later.

The bridge at the old creamery was built in the late 1700s. The prosperity of the O'Callaghan family of Old Shanbally House led to the construction of new roads (Smyth, 1976). The roads around Old Shanbally House, which lead to Burncourt, Clogheen, Ballylooby and Ballyporeen, were made around 1791–95.

The Top Road

The road between Cahir and Mitchelstown (the former N8) was probably built around 1794. William Smyth (1976) records the road as a turnpike road, which suggests that there may have been toll gates. The bridges, including the large bridge at Glengarra Wood, were built at this time. The bridge at Glengarra was built from cut limestone and had three arches, with intermediary decorative cutwaters, or piers, between the arches. Works on the bridge in early 2000 changed the architecture of the bridge and much of the detailed stonework was obliterated.

The M8

This was built from 2006–2008 and reduced the volume of traffic on the old N8.

11

The Famine

PRIOR TO THE FAMINE, the Burncourt area was much more densely populated than today, and most were small landowners, renting their holdings from the three major landowners – Viscount Lismore of Shanbally, the Buckleys of Galtee Castle and the Charteris of Cahir. Ed O'Riordan (1995) shows in his study *Famine in the Valley* that 24 per cent of the farms were 1–5 acres and 55 per cent were 5–30 acres. The remaining holdings were larger, ranging from 30–60 acres. The vast majority of people survived on a plot of ground and the diet was potatoes; only one in twenty had other work outside, such as farm labouring or cutting and selling turf for fuel or fertiliser.

Potato blight rotted crops in Europe and America in 1844 and spread to Ireland by 1845. This was devastating in a country where most of the population relied on potatoes for sustenance. The Famine hit South Tipperary in 1845 and the lack of potatoes, which was the staple food, left most of the population starving. The Famine was equally catastrophic in the Burncourt area. Robert Davis of the Society of Friends (Quakers) visited Burncourt in February 1847. Ed O'Riordan quotes from Davis's account of his trip around Clogheen, Burncourt and Skeheenarinky. Davis was trying to assess the level of starvation in 1847 and wrote of Burncourt:

> From Clogheen we proceeded to the village of Burncourt where destitution abounds to a fearful degree … deaths from actual starvation were becoming a daily occurrence; whilst the corpses were buried in some instances at night and without coffins.

Davis also records that he was gratified to see 'A well regulated and well supplied porridge shop now at work in the little village of Burncourt.' Davis continued his journey to the foot of the Galtee Mountains, where he also documented a desolate and wretched district. Davis noted at the end of his report that he was alarmed at the abandonment of land, particularly in the district from Burncourt to Tincurry, which was 'desolate and uncultivated'. Relief for the destitute during the Famine in Burncourt was in part provided by Mrs Grubb of Clashleigh House in Clogheen, who set up a Ladies Association and provided soup and porridge kitchens from late 1846, including the porridge shop in Burncourt which was mentioned by Davis. Many undoubtedly ended up in the workhouse in Clogheen. O'Riordan records that there were ongoing evictions of tenants who could not pay their rent, and for them the workhouse was the only option; these evictions, however, were not on the estate of Lord Lismore.

Relief schemes
Poor Law relief schemes were set up to provide work for the destitute. The schemes included roadworks and bridge repairs. Ed O'Riordan lists the schemes in the valley between the Galtee and Knockmealdown mountain ranges as including bridge repair at Shanrahan. The works also included building a boundary wall along the north side of the Top Road from the bridge at Glengarra to Brackbawn. The cost was not to exceed £50, which in today's monetary value is about £4,800 (€5380). It is not clear if the wall was ever built and nothing of it now survives, as the road has been considerably widened and raised over the past fifty years. The Cahir–Mitchelstown road was the mail-coach road from Dublin to Cork at the time and important for communication within the country.

The Schools Folklore Collection (Chapter 24) was compiled in 1937–39 by the pupils of Skeheenarinky National School and based on stories told to the children by older people in the district. Accounts of how the potatoes went blue and rotted after they were dug were written down. There are also some descriptions of Poor Law relief schemes. Pat Murphy, aged 54 in 1937, heard from his grandmother that the Black Road was made as part of a work scheme during the Famine. Tradition in the area confirmed that during the Famine men travelled daily on the Black Road to the Galtees and broke stones; Ard-na-Sglitha was referred to as a stone source. The pay per day was a pint of yellow meal (also known as 'Indian meal') which was collected in Griffith's in Ballyporeen; another account stated that workers got 4 lbs of meal every evening at Mr Jacksons. Hundreds of people queued for the meal. Michael Slattery, aged 58 years in 1937, heard from his father that during the Famine people worked for 4d. (2 cents, which is equivalent to €1.45 in today's monetary value) per day. Bridget Fitzgerald (née Leonard) recounted how she was told that during the Famine people were given three ha'pence for the hip of a mouse.

Other Famine stories

Mary Walshe, Coolagarranroe, recounted that all the spuds rotted on a man living in Ballyporeen. He had no sets (seed potatoes) and did not let on to the neighbours that he was so poor. He gathered a *máilín* (bag) of small stones and sat them. When he was setting them, he shook holy water on every *sciolán* (seed potato). When the time came to dig them, he had the best potatoes in the county. Mary Walshe also recounted evictions where tenants could not pay the rent.

Thomas Casey, aged 54 in 1937, told of a man stealing sticks; he got a month in Limerick Jail. When he returned home, his house was locked-up and his wife and children were in Clogheen Workhouse. A man caught killing a sheep was arrested and he and his wife were transported to Van Diemen's Land (Tasmania, Australia), where he became very rich.

Patrick Griffin of Clogheen, who was 75 years of age at the time of the Schools Folklore Collection, recounted that many ruined houses in the district were those of people who had either died during the Famine or emigrated to America. When the potatoes failed, some farmers had yellow meal stirabout. The meal was also bad, turning black when it was taken out of the pot. The poor ate grass and died in their hundreds by the roadsides. The poor tried to get work from farmers for a bit to eat, but seldom got it. The government relief schemes gave some men work making roads and tilling reas (marginal land) at a half-crown per perch. Patrick Griffin's grandfather tilled two perches and got 5s.

Population decline

The effect of the Famine in the Burncourt area was considerable; Ed O'Riordan records that the population dropped from 1,929 in 1841 to 1,280 in 1851, or almost 60 per cent of what it was. This was probably due to both emigration and death from starvation. O'Riordan suggests that the population may have been greater, as some of the landlords were unaware of the exact numbers of tenants on their estates. The number of inhabited houses also dropped from 322 houses in 1841 to 214 in 1851. O'Riordan estimates that 6,000 people died in the Clogheen/Burncourt area from the Famine, and a further 6,000 emigrated. His figures for the Burncourt area include a drop in population in the following: in Ballyhurrow, from 227 (1841) to 83 (1851) and houses inhabited reduced from 44 (1841) to 13 (1851); in Boolakennedy, from 128 inhabitants (1841) to 34 (1851) and houses reduced from 27 (1841) to 7 (1851); in Glengarra, from 214 (1841) to 82 (1851) and houses reduced from 40 (1841) to 16 (1851); and in Burncourt village, from 195 (1841) to 144 (1851) and houses reduced from 35 (1841) to 25 (1851). This drop in population was also partly due to the clearance of small landholders, and whole families left the area. These figures show a massive loss of people in areas of what was marginal land (('reas') that extended into the foothills of the Galtees; land that was brought into cultivation due to the huge rise in population before the Famine. The potato ridges can still be seen across the mountain.

12

Evictions and Move to the Mountain Slopes

IN MANY of the large estates in Ireland in the early nineteenth century, evictions took place for several reasons, but primarily when rent went unpaid and also because the landlord wanted to create larger, more profitable farms. When the Napoleonic Wars ended, prices for agricultural produce slumped and this caused a shortfall in income for the landed gentry. Smyth (1976) mentions an account sent by the Shanbally estate agent to Cornelius O'Callaghan, Viscount Lismore on the difficulty of collecting rent in 1817–1830. At that stage O'Callaghan still retained the lavish lifestyle and family commitments of the boom times in agriculture in the years 1790–1815. O'Callaghan was eventually forced to mortgage part of his estate for £100,000 (about £8.5 million in today's money). The farms were small (63 per cent were under 15 acres) and possibly inefficient. The policy of making bigger landholdings also resulted in farmers being forced off their farms.

Those dispossessed of their farms were forced to move to the slopes of the Galtee Mountains. This happened on all the estates which held land around Burncourt – on land held by Viscount Lismore of Shanbally, the Buckleys of Galtee Castle and the Charteris of Cahir. Those who moved upland were given some inducements, including reduced rents and subsidies for building houses, stone walls and limekilns. Limekilns on the foothills of the Galtees, including one in Glengarra Wood, probably date to the early 1800s. The construction of stone walls, which are still a feature of the landscape on the upper (north) side of Burncourt (Fig. 45), had the dual use of creating field boundaries and clearing the stones from the land. The road between Cahir and Mitchelstown was built around 1794 and many of the new farms were created along the line of this road.

In 1878, George Cornelius O'Callaghan, Viscount Lismore of Shanbally owned 34,945 acres in South Tipperary. When times were good the tenants were able to pay rent; when times were bad, rent remained unpaid. Poor weather and

FIG. 45–STONE WALLS ON THE NORTH SIDE OF BURNCOURT.

harvests in 1877–79 left the tenants poor if not destitute. The National Land League was established in the west of Ireland in 1876 to promote the cause of tenant farmers and ensure 'Fair Rent, Fixity of Tenure and Free Sale'. The Land League was set up in South Tipperary in 1879 to help tenant farmers. It was suppressed in 1881 and replaced by the Ladies' Land League, of which there was a branch in Burncourt. Ms Cashin of Burncourt Castle was the branch secretary. One of the functions of the Ladies' Land League was to provide material assistance to evicted tenants. The ladies were especially vociferous on the point of evictions and displayed anti-English sentiments. James O'Shea (1983) records that one Land League woman from Burncourt was quoted, in the Tipperary newspapers, in October 1882 as saying that the government got a 'slap in the face' with the election of the Fenian leader O'Donovan Rossa, who became an MP for the Tipperary constituency in a by-election in 1869. A land act introduced by Gladstone in 1881 conceded to the Land League's demands and paved the way for tenant security.

13

Christmas on the Galtees

WILLIAM O'BRIEN'S 1878 account of conditions on the Galtees, which was published in the *Freeman's Journal*, is of the hardship and poverty endured by the tenants on the Buckley estate, who owned Galtee Castle (Fig. 46). The lands were formerly part of the Kingston estate, which was placed in receivership in 1844 and bought by John Sadlier, MP, a banker in Thurles who himself became bankrupt in 1856. The estate was bought by Nathaniel Buckley in 1873, a cotton mill owner from Lancashire. Patten Smith Bridge was appointed as land agent

FIG. 46–GALTEE CASTLE, SKEHEENARINKY.

and he lived at Galtee Castle, a former hunting lodge built by the Kingstons in the 1780s. Smith Bridge was greedy and had no qualms about evicting tenants who could not pay the rent, which had increased by up to 500 per cent.

James Rourke, aged 40 years in 1937, recorded for the Schools Folklore Collection that when landlords (and he was referring to the Buckleys of Galtee Castle) wanted a farmer's land, rent payments were not accepted, the sheriff was called and the tenant was evicted. James Rourke recalled that in about 1870, Buckley's agent, Patten Smith Bridge, was very severe and refused to take the rent from a tenant-farmer named Ryan, who lived in Ballyporeen. Ryan was furious and decided to shoot Smith Bridge, lying in ambush on the road from Loughanna to Galtee Castle. When Smith Bridge approached, Ryan fired and Smith Bridge fell on the road but was unharmed, as he wore a steel jacket. Ryan then set off for America. Ryan's neighbours later hired an assassin named Thomas Crow, who lived in Co. Tipperary and was a 'noted landlord killer'. Smith Bridge was shot by Crow between Kilbehenny and Mitchelstown, but he again feigned death and fell to the ground, protected by his steel jacket. His driver Hyland was fatally wounded. Crow ran through the fields and rested in a ditch, where he fell asleep. Smith Bridge went to the police in Mitchelstown and they came out to the area and found Crow. Crow was brought to Galtee Castle, tried and executed. Another story from James Rourke concerned a farmer named John Murphy who went to pay his rent but this was not accepted. He was evicted and then threatened the Buckleys and their agents. The Buckleys gave him a small sum of money and he went to America.

Smith Bridge was denounced by the Fenian John Sarsfield Casey (1846–1896) for his treatment of the tenantry on the Buckley estate and William O'Brien was sent to examine the tenants' grievances. O'Brien travelled to the Buckley estate during Christmas of 1877 and early 1878 in the company of Very Rev. Dr Delaney, PP, Ballyporeen. The townlands O'Brien visited included Brackbawn, Skeheenarinky, Boolakennedy and Burncourt; he also visited the Mitchelstown Caves. William O'Brien was shaken by the destitution and wrote on 6 March 1878 that he left the estate of Nathaniel Buckley:

> in despair of ever being able to adequately to put before the eyes of the public, for their pity and indignation, the shameful scenes which passed under my eyes, in a time of peace, and in the name of the law.

There were 517 tenants on the estate, which comprised 22,000 acres extending from Araglin, Co. Tipperary to Anglesborough, Co. Limerick. The condition of the tenantry was appalling and many had been served with eviction notices.

O'Brien cited examples in Skeheenarinky which included Michael Dwyer whose rent was raised from £1 2s. 4d. to £1 15s. and part of whose land was taken to be attached to the schoolhouse. Patrick Burke's rent was raised from £4 18s. 7d. to £8, Darby O'Mahony's rent went from £2 to £4 and Michael O'Regan's from £5 9s. 6d. to £15 16s. 6d. The tenants also suffered if they tried to improve their lands, as the valuation was immediately increased and rents were raised. One man, James Hyland, was summonsed for gathering heath (heather) off the mountain and sent for seven days hard labour in Clonmel jail.

William O'Brien described the condition of the houses in Skeheenarinky and elsewhere as very basic; some of them were no more than hovels. O'Brien wrote of Mrs Johanna Fitzgerald, whose husband had gone to England as a labourer to earn money to feed the family. Mrs Fitzgerald had 1s. left to feed her family at Christmas. In O'Brien's diary on 24 December 1877 he recounted that 'I thought it my duty to repair to Mountain Lodge [Galtee Castle] to lay before Mr. Bridge [the land agent] a frank statement on what I had seen.' Mr Bridge had, however, gone to Roscrea for Christmas. O'Brien wrote, on St Stephen's Day (26 December 1877), that 'my head almost swims with tales of misery, poverty, squalor and despair poured into my ears from fifty different sources'. He also wrote, 'I saw enough around the Galtees to make my heart bleed.' He contrasted the poor Christmas meal of the Buckley tenants with that enjoyed in Mitchelstown Workhouse. Buckley tenants were semi-starved.

John Sarsfield Casey had been imprisoned on Spike Island and in Cork jails and was convicted of treason and felony in December 1865, resulting in his transportion to Australia in 1867. He was pardoned and returned to Ireland in 1870. Writing under the nom-de-plume of 'The Galtee Boy' Sarsfield Casey recorded the poverty on the Buckley estate in an article in the *Cork Examiner* on 13 April 1878. He was very familiar with Skeheenarinky and the Buckley estate, as his father's business in Mitchelstown dealt in hides, feathers and eggs, and some of his suppliers were from Skeheenarinky; the Buckley tenants also went to Mitchelstown fairs and shopped in the town. He wrote, 'how the inhabitants live there [Carrigeen] obtain food here, much less pay rent is a mystery to most people as the holdings consist of tracts of heath'. He noted that some rents had increased by 500 per cent, citing Maurice Fitzgerald whose rent rose from £1 18s. 6d. to £6 10s. and Patrick McNamara, his rent rising from £3 6s. to £17 12s. In a further article in the *Cork Examiner*, also in 1878 Sarsfield Casey wrote that the diet was mainly potatoes dipped in a little new milk with a pinch of salt.

An article in the *Freeman's Journal* on 14 December records that Sarsfield Casey was accused of a criminal libel action on Mr Patten Smith Bridge.

Accounts at Sarsfield Casey's trial record again the huge rent rises imposed by Patten Smith Bridge on behalf of the Buckley estate. Edmond Darney, a farmer aged 40 years from Coolagarranroe, made a deposition saying his rent rose from £2 6s. to £4 6s. Terence Murphy, a farmer aged 38 years, stated that his rent rose from £3 5s. to £7 7s. 9d.; Thomas Kearney, a farmer aged 46 years, stated that his rent rose from £5 12s. 6d. to £17 10s. Thomas Hyland, a farmer aged 50 years from Skeheenarinky, stated that he had worked hard reclaiming land and the tenants had to draw manure to the fields on their backs as they did not own a horse and cart.

14

Police and Military Barracks

TIPPERARY, as a county, was a volatile region in Ireland, prone to rebellion, and as a consequence it was heavily populated with armed forces. Clogheen was one of the garrison towns where the Tipperary militia were based, and there were many other small posts scattered around South Tipperary. The militia had the dual role of soldier and policeman, as there was no police force throughout the 1700s; this situation continued on into the 1800s. The Irish Constabulary was established in 1822 and became the Royal Irish Constabulary in 1867.

Burncourt village
The Old Shanbally Bar was formerly an RIC barracks, which was in use before the 1840s, as it is recorded in the 1840 Ordnance Survey as a police barracks (Fig. 47). It ceased as a barracks sometime between 1840 and 1905, and became a shop and public house owned by the Ryan family.

FIG. 47–FORMER RIC BARRACKS IN BURNCOURT VILLAGE.

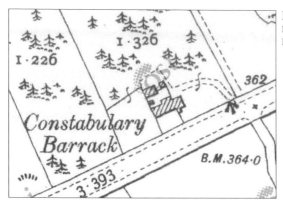

FIG. 48–ORDNANCE SURVEY (1905) RECORD OF THE CONSTABULARY BARRACK IN GLENGAR.

Glengar

The police barracks in Glengar (Fig. 48) was in use when the 1911 Census was taken. The RIC members stationed at the barracks were unnamed. The 1911 Census only records that there was a sergeant from Co. Galway, aged 34, and four constables, aged 25–31, who were from Cork, Roscommon, Limerick and Kerry.

FIG. 49–REHILL POLICE BARRACKS.

Rehill

Rehill is not recorded on the Ordnance Survey maps as a police barracks (Figs 49–51). The garrison is listed by David J. Butler (2006) as a constabulary station in 1830–32, and as having a cohort of one constable and three sub-constables. Rehill Barracks was in use as a barracks and military station during the War of Independence. The barracks had eight policemen in 1920. The Black and Tans were also stationed on site, but the local policemen refused to allow them access to the barracks and they had to camp nearby.

FIG. 50–REHILL POLICE BARRACKS, PORCH WITH GUN LOOP PROTECTING EXTERNAL WALL.

FIG. 51–REHILL POLICE BARRACKS, GUN LOOP INSIDE PORCH.

15

The National Schools

THE NINETEENTH–CENTURY background to the first schools was the desire by the government, the Catholic Church and local landlords to provide some type of rudimentary education to the poor of Ireland. The backdrop to the mid-nineteenth century was the Famine, whereby the whole population suffered to some extent and, through starvation and latterly emigration, its number plummeted.

The children attending Burncourt School were largely from the locality and the roll books list the townlands from which they came. Some of the addresses are incorrect in that children may, in fact, have been from neighbouring townlands. An example of this is Rehill townland, which is given for many pupils though they came from adjoining townlands such as Ballyhurrow, Glengar and Boolakennedy. Most of the records in the National Archives are in the form of inspector's reports and payments made to the school for small sums for requisites.

History of primary education

The Penal Laws (from 1695) forbade Catholics many civil rights, including education; these laws were relaxed and eventually repealed in 1778 and 1782. The only schooling available to Catholics was pay schools, or hedge schools, where the pupils paid a small fee to attend. These schools were illegal and classes were initially held in hedgerows, on byways and, later, in cabins or sheds. By the turn of the nineteenth century, hedge schools were operating openly; there were three of these schools recorded in the Burncourt area in the early 1800s. A Church of Ireland system of parochial schools operated in Ireland, but these were not attended by Catholics. Poverty also precluded many children from any formal education, as the fee for pay schools was beyond the means of most. The Christian Brothers, founded by Edmund Rice, opened schools for the poor from

74

the 1820s onwards, but they were mainly situated in urban centres.

Schools were also part of the workhouses set up for the destitute, but in pre-Famine times access to these schools was only for the workhouse inmates; one had to be destitute to gain entry into the workhouse, where conditions were miserable. A workhouse was opened in the district of Clogheen in 1842; Ed O'Riordan records in his book, *Famine in the Valley* (1995), that the first schoolmaster was Richard Burke, who was paid £15 per year, and the first schoolmistress was Mary Nowlan.

There was concern amongst the Catholic bishops about hedge schools, as they had no say in the schools and there was no control over the standard of education. The British Government was concerned because it was felt that anti-British sentiment could be promoted in the schools. The Irish Catholic bishops petitioned the government to enquire into the state of education in Ireland in 1824. The government was happy to set up the enquiry, because it would give them some control over Catholic education. The growing population of pre-Famine Ireland in the early 1800s necessitated some educational policy on behalf of the British Government. A commission was set up to enquire into the state of education in Ireland and the National Education Board was established by Lord Stanley in 1831. The board's function was to fund primary education, offering grant-aid for school buildings, teachers' salaries and the establishment of teacher-training colleges.

National schools were set up and commissioners appointed. These commissioners were to administer 'funds placed at the disposal of his Excellency, The Lord Lieutenant, for the education of the poor of Ireland'. They received applications for aid towards the building and fitting-up of schools, the paying of teachers and the obtaining of books and school requisites. The conditions for applications were listed as follows:

- Local funds were to be raised for annual repair of the schoolhouse and furniture, and for teachers' salaries, books and school requisites.
- At least one third of funding for the schoolhouse building was to be covered by funds raised locally.
- A certain number of hours were to be set aside for religious education. The clergy were to give instruction, either before or after ordinary school hours.
- The commissioners were to retain control over school books. No religious books were to be used in the school.
- A school register was to be kept and attendance and non-attendance of each child was to be marked on divine days of worship, or Sundays.

- All teachers had to receive previous instruction in a model school in Dublin.
- All teachers were liable to be fined, suspended or removed when commissioners deemed it necessary.
- Commissioners or inspectors were to be allowed to visit the school.

In these early days of primary education, there was an obligation on the local community to partly fund the schools. This continues into the present, where parents are obliged to pay the capitation fee. Religious instruction was excluded from the curriculum as the emphasis was on non-denominational education. The basic code of the schools is recorded in the archive of the Commissioners of Education as a lesson from St Paul:

> Live peaceably with all men. Love one another behave gently and kindly to everyone.

One of the main objectives of the government was to provide non-denominational education so as to unite children of different creeds in one system; this depended upon the co-operation of the resident clergy. The Commissioners of Education looked with particular favour upon applications from:

- A Protestant clergyman and Roman Catholic clergyman acting jointly.
- A clergyman of one denomination and a certain number of laymen of the other.
- Laymen of both denominations.

The training colleges, known as 'model schools', were only in Dublin, but because of the demand for training, model schools were eventually opened in each province. The model school in Cork is close to City Hall and is still in use as a courthouse. The model schools were banned by the Catholic clergy, however, because of their secular teaching; this only resulted in a lack of trained teachers. The Powis Commission of 1870 recommended that denominational education be allowed, and this resulted in mostly separate education for Catholics and Protestants. The model schools were replaced by teacher-training colleges in 1883, where teachers for Catholic schools were trained.

The emphasis of the curriculum was on the 'three R's': reading, writing and arithmetic, with spelling and tables learned by rote. The overall benefit was a huge reduction in illiteracy rates. English was taught and many felt this was more useful than Irish. Irish history was introduced as a subject in 1842. It was not until after the emergence of the Irish Free State in 1922 that Irish was taught in primary schools for one hour per day, and history, geography and singing were also taught through Irish.

Attendance was at the discretion of the parents and, as many children were needed for farm work, their attendance at school may have been determined by the needs of the farming community. It was only in 1892 that attendance for all children aged 6–14 became compulsory.

There was initially no formal exam at the end of primary school. A written exam in Irish, English and arithmetic, known as the Primary Certificate, was introduced in 1929, but this was optional; it became compulsory from 1943–1969, until it was dropped as part of the assessment system.

The old school

An application by Fr Matthius Casey for funding of primary schools in Burncourt was received by the Commissioners of Education on 17 March 1841. The application was for two schools – a boys' school and a girls' school (Fig. 52). A blank application form was dispatched on 19 March 1841 by the commissioners, and this was returned by Fr Casey on 27 March 1841. The application was allocated two numbers, Nos 3019 and 3020, and was for two schools to be housed in the same building; No 3019 referred to the boys' school and No 3020 referred to the girls' school.

The merits of the proposed school were reported on by the superintendent

FIG. 52–THE OLD SCHOOL (NOW COMMUNITY CENTRE).

for the Commissioners of the Board of Education in 1841. The signatures on the report were from three commission secretaries, Thomas Casey (Clogheen), Hamilton Dowdall, and another name that is partly obliterated from the document in the National Archive records, but may be 'Maurice Cropper'. The report states that the proposed school is:

> Situated at the village of Burncourt in the Parish of Ballysheehan, townland of Burncourt in the Barony of Iffa and Offa West, County of Tipperary. Permission to make lease of site from Cornelius Lord Viscount Lismore of Shanbally Castle. Length of lease is to be three lives of 31 years at a rent of one shilling per year. The names of the proposed trustees were – The Very Reverend Matthius Casey PP of Clogheen and Burncourt, The Right Reverend, Doctor Nicholas Foran, The Catholic Bishop of Waterford and Lismore and Lord Viscount of Lismore.

The report goes on as follows:

> Taking the population as a rule, in this locality I would say that 400 children made up of male and female would generally attend. Two school rooms would be required, the upper floor for females, the lower floor for boys under the same roof.

The school envisaged was a two-storey building; in fact, the school was built as a single-storey with the boys and girls in separate sections.

The report continues:

> There are two schools at present, if approved of by the inspector; I trust you will grant a salary and books, besides £120 in cash. I expect £30 more in labour from man and horse.

The cost of £120 was a considerable outlay in 1841; in today's terms it was about €12,800. A superintendent's report on the schoolhouse on 11 May 1841 was in the scheme of a question and answer form. In the report, the proposed school was described as being on one acre of land, adjoining the village of Burncourt, and being 'in a healthy situation'. This probably means that it was in open countryside, away from any industrial area such as a quarry or farmyards. The site was described as being enclosed, with a stone wall on three sides and an iron railing on the fourth side. This is very much as it is today, with the iron railing being replaced by a stone wall. The proposed school was also described as being unconnected with any chapel, church or meeting house, or any other religious establishment.

The lease for the site was from Lord Lismore, and the lease was of indefinite duration and not liable to rent. Lord Lismore, the Rev. Matthius Casey, PP of Burncourt and Clogheen, and Dr Foran, Catholic Bishop of Waterford and Lismore were the school trustees. These individuals raised possibly £100, which was already available for the school building project in 1841. The function of the trustees was to maintain the school, and they were consequently responsible for the building and the repairs. The families of those attending were also expected to make some subscriptions for school repairs.

The expected number of pupils was in the region of 250 males and 150 females. A file in the National Archives relating to Burncourt School archive records a population of 6,000 in the vicinity of Burncourt, but this may include areas outside the immediate village, as a population figure of 1,929 was recorded by the Census Commission in the early 1840s. The commission secretaries, Thomas Casey, Hamilton Dowdall and Maurice Cropper (?), may have only assumed the high population.

The question of religious instruction was also addressed in the application from Fr Casey and his report on the village stated that 'at present there are none but Roman Catholic clergymen in the neighbourhood'. Arrangements for the religious instruction of other denominations were to be made locally. As there is little information on the pupils attending the school, the number of Church of Ireland and Presbyterian pupils is unknown. It was expected that some of the children from the Shanbally and Glengall estates would attend, and some of these children were certainly Church of Ireland or Presbyterian. The record of graves in Ballysheehan church, with names such as Sheridan and Clepenarch, shows that the population included non-Catholic members. In later years, a number of children – surnames including Hays, McCulloch, Munroe and Heuston – were also either Church of Ireland or Presbyterian.

The report signed by the commission secretaries also emphasised the need for a school in Burncourt and stated:

There being no school for the poor within a circuit of 4–5 miles of the neighbourhood the necessity of establishing one is too apparent to require explanation.

A school's inspector visited Burncourt and his report concluded:

I have never visited an applicant school in the establishment of which so much anxiety was evinced by the peasantry. Such ideas may be formed of its interest from the amount of funds (£150) subscribed in one fortnight by the poor people for the erection of the house. The children from the estates of Lord Lismore and Glengal [*sic*] being likely to form the majority of those in attendance is as expected, these noblemen will assist in the management and support the school when established. This application deserves in my opinion to be attended to.

The sequence of the building of the schools is recorded in the National Archives, and a grant of £130 was sanctioned in June 1841, including £6 for privies (toilets). The expected number of pupils was 255 and the ground was to be leased for three lives or 31 years. There appear to have been some delays to the building's construction; the project was granted an extension to the construction programme to September. A record in the National Archives shows that the building cost was £300 and of that £171 was through grant-aid for the building, a grant of £20 was for fitting up and £109 was raised locally. The board paid the money on 11 February 1843 and the trustees may have had to cover the costs until the grant was paid – some things never change! The teachers' salaries were set at £8 per year. Requisites, which were presumably similar to those in the workhouse school in Clogheen, were listed as paper, ink, inkstands, quills, slates and slate pencils, and were also financed by the Commissioners for Education; in December 1842, a sum of £4 was paid for these to the Burncourt school. Requisites payments continued throughout the school's history and were normally paid quarterly. For example, in January 1844 the following sums were sent by the Board of Education: December, £2 1s. 4d.; May, £2 19s. 2d.; July, £2 8s. 2d.; September, £1 7s. 6d.; November, £1 12s. 11d. Books for 150 pupils were sent in 1842.

A further application on December 1842 dealt with the teachers for the boys' and girls' schools. The teachers had already been in place since March and April, and this merely sanctioned their appointments. Both schools were treated separately in the official documentation, although both were housed in the same building.

Boys' school

The proposed boys' school teacher was Philip McGrath. He was aged 36 and from the locality. He had not attended a model school and had never taught in a school, but he was recommended by the trustees and he was also described as being 'a native of the parish who has been to school'. The school opened in March

1842 and the boys' section was one classroom, 44' x 21', with an attendance of 142 males, expected to rise to 160. The donations from the scholars were also recorded in the archive as farthings (¼d.) and halfpennies (½d.) per quarter. Philip McGrath died in 1845 after just two and a half years in the job. A teacher named as 'M. Riordan' was in place from 1846–47, but he was absent from May–September 1846 and a temporary teacher was appointed.

Girls' school

The girls' school opened in April 1842. The first teacher in the girls' school was Margaret Kavanagh, aged 19, who lived to the north of the Top Road (N8) in Glengar townland. She wasn't trained and had never taught in a school, but was recommended by the superintendent. The girls' school was 30' x 21' x 10' and comprised of one classroom with forty-eight girls in attendance. This was expected to rise to 120.

Assistant teachers (monitors)

The teaching system included the use of monitors and the first of these in the girls' school was Margaret Riordan and Eliza Kavanagh. The monitors in the boys' school are not recorded as such, although the Board of Education sent a letter in September 1845 to cancel the salary awarded to James Callaghan as a paid monitor from October 1845 as he did not discharge his duties properly. A grant of £4 was made out to Edward Flynn as a paid monitor from 1 February 1846, having acted in the place of the missing Callaghan.

History of the school from 1840–1940

The Famine hit the entire country and was equally bad in the Burncourt area. This must have had a severe impact on the school, including the teachers and pupils. It is against this backdrop that the school was trying to establish itself as an educational resource, and it is probable that few pupils attending did not experience some hardship. In Burncourt the population in 1841 was recorded as 1,929 and by 1851 this had dropped to 1,280; 322 houses were occupied in 1841, but this was reduced to 214 in 1851. The drop in population must also have reduced the numbers in school.

The history of Burncourt school from the 1850s is recorded mainly from notes on payments and changes of personnel. On 18 June 1850 the school manager Rev. James Kelly, PP notified the Board of Education of the resignation of Julia O' Grady and the appointment of Julie Daly. Julia O'Grady had resigned by early November 1850. She appears to have come back to the school, as she is listed as a monitor in 1852 alongside a new teacher named Hanora Daly whose salary was £13. In 1852 the boys' school teacher was William Moloney and his salary was £22. There was obviously no pay parity here! A letter in September 1852 notified the Board of Education of the resignation of a teacher named 'P. Butler'.

In April 1853 the schools' inspector reported that a teacher in Burncourt communicated with the government. The inspector suspected that there was meddling in political matters and received the sum of £3 as a reward for some recent information. The reply to this report was that the commissioners did not feel called upon to interfere, as the nature of the correspondence with the government to which he alluded was merely conjectural. The commissioners obviously didn't want to get involved with local affairs!

In 1854 the school manager notified the board of the resignation of Michael Cantwell, who emigrated, and James Ryan was subsequently appointed. By 1855 the manager had appointment a 'C.M. O'Brien' as the teacher. This was not sanctioned, however, as the commissioners considered that charges against O'Brien and his character made him unsuitable. The attendance of boys in the 1860s was, on average, between sixty-six and seventy.

The teacher in the girls' school was Susan McInery in the early 1860s; her assistant teacher was Mary Keogh and the monitor was Anne Lonergan. Mary Keogh was quite young; her age is given as eighteen and a half. The number of girls attending the school was ninety-two, with an average attendance of sixty-two.

The boys' and girls' schools were amalgamated in 1899 when the Board of Education recommended that Burncourt Boys NS be struck off the roll of National Schools from 31 December 1897; from this date, it was superseded by Burncourt Mixed National School, No 3020. This roll number remains in use today. The schools were amalgamated for one year, on trial, on 1 January 1898, because the boys' school teacher, Mr Michael Duggan, retired on a gratuity from 1 December 1897. Mrs Duggan, his wife, was placed in charge of the mixed school. The amalgamation was sanctioned in 1899 'in view of the very efficient manner in which it was conducted during past year'. Mrs Duggan continued as principal until 1902, when she was replaced by John O'Callaghan. An interesting fact about Mrs Duggan is that she was remembered as an excellent teacher and also taught several boys who were later to form part of the flying column in Burncourt during the War of Independence, including Denis Lonergan (Burncourt), Bill and Ned Mulcahy (the caves) and Jack Ryan (Boolakennedy).

The roll books in Burncourt began in 1891 for the boys' school and 1887 for the girls' school. Up to 1892 there was no obligation on the teachers to keep rolls, as it was only then that school attendance became compulsory. The roll books record the year a child started. In all, 693 girls attended the school between 1887–2006 and 769 boys attended between 1891–2006, giving a total of 1,462. There may have been up to 1,000 pupils in the years between the school opening in 1842 until the roll was first taken in the late 1880s. Apart from the start date, the roll books list the fathers' occupations and these were in the main farmers and labourers. The labourers may have worked on farms, the roads or forestry, or on the Shanbally estate. Other occupations included craftsmen (tailor, shoemaker, smith, mason, sawyer, baker), estate-workers (caretaker, gamekeeper, herdsman, domestic servant, gardener, steward), policemen, teachers, shopkeepers, timber merchants, travellers and railway officials. The children attending the school came from a variety of backgrounds.

Mr O'Callaghan began teaching in 1902 and continued until 1947. His wife Mollie (née English) taught alongside him; Mollie retired in 1940, as females were required to retire when they reached 60 years of age.

Teachers in the old school, Burncourt

1950s

Diarmuid O'Dea, Principal (1953–?); Anne Leamy (1959–?); Alma Whelan (1958); Eibhlín Flemming (1958); Claire Breen (1955–1958); Pauline Griffin (1954–1955); Margaret Egar (1953–1954); Kathleen O'Leary (1953); Mary O'Callaghan (1952–1953); Mary Fitzgerald (1949–1952).

1930s–1940s

John O'Callaghan, Principal (1902–1946); James Daly, Principal (1946–1953); William Ahearne (1940–1947); Bridget English (1910–1949); Mollie English (?–1940).

1842–1899

Mary English (1899–?); Bridie English (?); Mrs. Conway (?); Mr Michael Duggan (?–1897); Mrs Duggan (?–1902); Susan McInery (early 1860s); C.M. O'Brien (?–1855); James Ryan (?–1854); Michael Cantwell (?–1859); P. Butler (?–1852); William Moloney (?–1852); Hanora Daly (1852–?); Catherine Daly (1850s); Julie Daly (1850s); Edward Flynn (1846); James Callaghan (1845); Philip McGrath (1842–1845); Margaret Kavanagh (1842–?); Margaret Riordan (1842–1847); Eliza Kavanagh (1842–?).

Memories from the old Burncourt school

The following are snippets of memories from former pupils of the old Burncourt national school. They were recorded in 2006, for the fiftieth anniversary of the construction of the new school. Some of the accounts show the frequent use of the stick.

Peg Cleary, Toormore

I started school in Burncourt in November 1927 when my family moved from Kenmare Co. Kerry. My brother Jerry and sister Hannah also attended the school, both being older than me. We had spent the first years in Ruscussane National School and came to Burncourt when my father took a job with the Shanbally Estate as a forester. The teachers in Burncourt were Jack O'Callaghan [principal] his wife Mollie and Bridie English who taught the infants. The subjects were reading, writing and sums and we also did Irish and Religion. Punishment was meted out regularly to the pupils. Mr. O'Callaghan used to go out to the school yard, smoked his pipe and cut sallies for use as a stick to beat the pupils. One pupil was slapped so hard that his hands bled and he [the pupil] used the blood to write his exercises – more punishment was given for that! One of my memories was when we were made to stand up and recite passages from the Bible. My friend Mary English had brought a bugán [an egg without a shell] to the school and she was about to put it up to my mouth as part of the caffling that went on, she missed my mouth and the egg broke and spread on the floor. I couldn't stop laughing and got to spend the rest of the day with my nose to the wall. Apart from slaps, our hair was pulled and we were lifted off the ground by the hair.

Most pupils stayed on until seventh class or about 13 or 14 years. One of the smartest in my class was George Heuston who went on to manage the bakery in Cahir. Some children from Shanbally Estate attended the school including the Munroes (Betty, Jean, John and Jessie) and Heustons. These were Protestant children who left the classroom when religion was taught.

The toilets were outdoor in the backyard of the school. We went outside for our breaks and mostly went down the village. At that time there were houses along the south side of the village where among the inhabitants were two sisters, the Miss Dobbins – Judy and another whose name I can't remember. Mrs Duggan had a shop at the end of the village and her husband Mikey had a forge. There was an old rhyme that went:

'Who built the world? Mikey Duggan with a spade and shovel.'

In summer, we went to school barefoot and I used to leave my shoes in the ditch at the top of the boreen and go barefoot to school. I put them on when I got back in the evening and went in home. We brought bundles of kindling to school in the winter for the fire and the boys were sent out to break sticks for the fire. There was an open fire in the school and this was the only heating.

For games we played in the school yard but mostly went down the village.

Mike Fox, Killavenogue

I started school at about six years old and in those days we didn't like the thought of being so confined. Discipline was very important, teachers were sterner and corporal punishment was the order of the day. Miss English was my first teacher. She had charge of the infants, first and second class. There were ten of us in the class, evenly matched, five boys and five girls, most of whom were still there when we left school.

When we got to first and second class, we would be sent out to the headmaster, Mr. O'Callaghan, a couple of evenings a week, as all the girls came into our room for sewing and knitting classes. In the meantime we had mental arithmetic with the Master, which was really great as it sharpened our minds. This was really very useful later in life when we bought a few items in a shop and had the total amount totted up very quickly. Needless to say, this was long before the advent of calculators and it was a case of using the head rather than a pencil.

In third and fourth class, our teacher was Mr. Aherne. He was a Wexford man and he had just replaced Mrs. O'Callaghan, who was the Master's wife. He used to play the bagpipes and was a very nice man but didn't stay very long in the area before moving back to his home place.

There wasn't any electricity in those days, so almost all the heating was provided by solid fuel. Most of my school years were during the War, so coal was also a scarce commodity. In the school, we had old stoves for heating and sometimes the older boys were asked to bring some timber for helping out with the fuel demands. Everybody loved doing this as it was a great excuse to stay away from school for a few hours, although it wouldn't do to prolong the job as the Master might be waiting with a stick!

Toilet facilities were also very old-fashioned and consisted of a plank of wood with a few circular holes cut in it. It is very hard to explain to young people today that we used this. Of course there was no water for flushing the 'toilets'. There was a story told that a small boy fell through one of the holes in the plank and had to be rescued. Hygiene was a word we didn't hear about and I believe children were far healthier in those days as they became immune to a lot of illnesses.

Money was also scarce, but a few pennies [240 to the £] would buy a lot. You could get four big biscuits for 1 penny at Guiry's Shop and also a penny's worth of sweets was quite substantial. Lunch consisted of a couple of cuts of homemade bread and butter and a bottle of milk. Occasionally we'd have some homemade sweet cake for a treat! All food came from home in those days and we had very little money.

Occasionally, we might have a fight between two budding 'Jack Dempseys' or 'Joe Louis', nothing too serious resulting in injuries like a thick lip or a black eye and all recovered to fight another day. The games we played were 'Burnt Ball', Rounders, Football and Hunts. The girls used to play a game called 'Trance' on the ground. A 'slig' or small stone was pushed or kicked from square to square by the player while hopping on one leg. If the slig landed on a line, you were out. Some of the boys were also quite adept at this game. We usually played against Clogheen in football. We used to walk to Clogheen on a Sunday for a match. Sometimes one lad had a donkey and car and we took turns, four or five at a time, driving in state!

We spent the last years in school with Mr. O'Callaghan and during that time we were taught how to serve Mass. It was very different from today, as we had to learn all the responses in Latin and I'm afraid I'll have to say, we were rather irreverent about some of the phraseology, as we hadn't a clue as to the meaning of the words. A whole lot of us would be trained together and eight or ten of us would serve Mass.

Mr. O'Callaghan was a great mathematician and in fact, taught us some algebra. There was generally a seventh class in those days and this was usually the end of their education for most people in my age group.

Denis Lonergan, Glengar

I went to school in the late 1930's and early 1940's and the teachers were Mr. O'Callaghan, his wife Mollie and Mrs. Conway. Mollie O'Callaghan retired in 1940 as she reached 60. Mr. O'Callaghan was a great teacher and taught extra subjects such as higher level maths and algebra. My early memories are of the First Communion when there was an intensive drive on religious instruction for about two weeks before the Communion. The teacher marched us down to the church where we all had a practice confession and the teacher would hear our confessions! When we were small we were sent out to the hall which was on Creed's side of the building and the senior girls taught us Catechism.

The school building was divided into two rooms; the big room was about 1½ times the size of the smaller one and there was a hall on the side of the small room where the coats were hung. A small blackboard hung in Mr. O'Callaghan's room where he added up the numbers attending school, which in my time were about 160.

We walked barefoot to school from May 1st to the end of September and some of the more hardy boys went barefoot until November. We had six weeks summer holidays from the last Friday in July to the second Monday

FIG. 53–BURNCOURT NATIONAL SCHOOL SIGN; SIGN PAINTED OVER DURING WORLD WAR II
AND TRACES OF WHITE PAINT REMAIN ON THE SIGN.

in September. The village had more houses when I was in school and there
was a small house opposite Creed's where Judy Dobbins lived. She is
remembered in the church as she donated the Holy Water Font.

I remember two young lads who lived in the village, named Joe and
Mickey Hall. At that time there was a band in the village under the
directorship of Tim Dowling. Mickey Hall was very musical and later joined
the army band, but he also said that his best music teacher was Tim Dowling.

During the War years extra pupils [Keoghs] came to the school as they
evacuated from Dublin after the bombings and lived with Mrs. Burke and
Stephen. A girl of the Munroes also returned to the school as she wasn't able
to travel to her Church of Ireland school. The War years saw the sign for the
school painted over in white (Fig. 53) and traces of the paint can be seen on
the sign [now in the Community Centre]. The idea behind this was that in
the event of a German invasion, the Germans wouldn't know where they
were. There was no shortage of exercise books, although the paper was very
poor quality and almost see-through. Ink was made up from powder and
water. I remember that the pupils were given tablets for goitre as the area was
supposed to be a bad area for this problem and most of the tablets ended up
in the ink-wells.

There was no electricity in those days but we didn't need it as it was bright in the rooms. Electricity didn't actually come to Burncourt until 1957/58. Boys from each area or along each road had to bring in firewood and we were able to spend hours away from school on this mission. The sticks were piled into a shed beside the school teachers' house and as far as we knew, the headmaster never checked the amount we brought.

We had about a half an hour for each subject and we learned a lot of poetry and English grammar from Mr. O'Callaghan. All the poems in a book called 'The Spirit of Tipperary' owned by Mr. O'Callaghan were learned by the senior classes. One of the boys wrote an essay for Mr. O'Callaghan on a trip to Dublin where he said he left at 9am on his father's bicycle and returned at 3pm having seen an All-Ireland Final, visited the National Museum and a bombing. All he really was trying to do was make a feck out of the teacher.

Bridie English walked home from school and we used to wait for her to go and then rob her orchard. She stopped at the 'Store' for messages one day, unknown to us and we got caught when she came on after us. The boys got slapped the day after.

Helen Kelly (née Butler), Glencallaghan

In 1942 I was taken to school with the Griffin family. Miss Bridie English was our first teacher in school. She gathered us like a clutch of chickens around her big wood-burning stove in the middle of the class room. There we learned our A, B, C, formed our figures 1, 2, 3, moulded the mala into hens nests and eggs. The boys made long worms.

Preparation for First Confession and Holy Communion was an intense course, taught with many questions and answers. Reverence and respect for the sacraments was unique. Communion Day was one of the happiest days of my life. Girls all in white dresses, veils and wreaths, holding a lighted candle surrounded by a ring of wild flowers. Boys wearing short-pants suits, collar and tie and a beautiful rosette on the left lapel. A can of boiled sweets was distributed to all of us by our teacher. School days at the age of seven progressed, learning Irish, English and Sums continued. Numbers must have increased, because in 2nd, 3rd and 4th class we had a Mr. Aherne teach us. Geography and history were added as subjects. Knitting and sewing classes were given to the girls, while the boys marched and played football in the yard.

In the back yard were the toilet facilities – Dry Toilets of course. Little ones were escorted there in case they fell in.

Mothers and ladies of the parish had a teacher come to give classes in dressmaking, cookery and crafts in the school at night. The V.E.C. provided this teacher of Domestic Science. The girls of 5th and 6th class were invited to an after-school class in cooking and embroidery. Alas, the quota of numbers was not there so we from 3rd and 4th joined in. The excitement was intense as we saw buns and scones rise in the oven – oil stoves then. There were mostly pot-ovens at home then, also known as 'bastibles'. My memory of the great snowfall in 1947 always brings to mind the Big Boys in school – Paddy and Benny Normoyle, John Connors and Pete Fehilly who took us girls, Peggy Griffin, Peggy Pyne, Breda Carey and myself over the snow drifts on a wooden plank. We still kept going to school as the snow lay on the ground for many weeks.

Cipíní [wooden twigs] were always brought to school when the winter weather came. These were used to light up the stove for heat. A good excuse for those of us coming from Glencallaghan, Crannagh, Ballysheehan and Cuillinagh to be late for school – 'Had to collect cippins in Tom Maher's Wood Sir'. Autumn time made it late getting home, as the boys had to go into the turnip field and pull a turnip or two, smashed it into pieces on the stone wall, while the girls looked on, but we all enjoyed scooping the lovely juicy sweet turnip (a source of iron) on our way home. Springtime was wild flower picking time for the girls to take into the teacher for the May Altar. The hedgerows were then covered with primroses and violets. Summer time delayed getting home, as we just had to have a paddle in the river, water had to be drunk from the well behind the stile by cupping our hands. The boys splashed us in the river with water but fortunately the sun dried our clothes before we got home. On wet days, fathers collected us in the horse drawn dray-car with a good bed of straw on the floor. All packed in for the ride home, old sacks and oil skins covered us.

In 5th and 6th class, a new master came to Burncourt. Mr. Daly from Castlebar, Co. Mayo. He was ginger-haired and hence a fiery man. He had some reformation to do. He was somebody who didn't suffer fools gladly and took no nonsense. He found lots of material in the pupils for learning, music and song talent in us Burncourt Folk. His wife, Helen, gave us violin lessons. The Master introduced us to tunes from shows like The White Horse Inn, Brigadoon and the Pirates of Penzance. Shows he and his wife had been to on their travels in Cork, Tipperary and Clonmel. Hence we developed a love and appreciation of music. First thing in the morning a round of mental arithmetic was the norm – to sharpen our brain. After lunch, twenty questions for 20 minutes put us thinking too. 'The meaning of Big Words' given daily was the Friday evening test, before we got out of school. Geography and History classes were made a reality when we went on our school outing by bus. Parents were welcome to come along. Memories of visiting Bansha Jam Factory developed by Canon Hayes, Muintir na Tire. Bunratty Castle – a picnic there on the grounds, a ruin as it was then in 1950 and on to Ardnacrusha Power Station. Other trips took us to Mount Mellery, Youghal and Lismore Castle.

The new school

The new school in Burncourt was opened in 1956. The land on which the school is sited was donated by Denis McGrath and he also gave the land for the new church and graveyard. The land was transferred from Denis McGrath's ownership in 1955 to the trustees, who are listed as Rev. Daniel Cohalan, Bishop of Waterford and Lismore, Rev. Canon Kelly, President of St John's College, Waterford, and Thomas Power, PP. The Minister for Education sanctioned a grant of £4,971 8s. 7d. for 'erecting the schoolhouse, and the finishing and furnishing thereof'. A sum of £828 11s. 5d. was raised locally by voluntary contribution. The school was built by Pyne's of Fermoy, who had also built the church in 1952. The building was too small to house the numbers and the old school was retained until an extension was built in 1963. A further extension was built in the 2000s under the direction of Pat O'Callaghan, principal from 1979. The present school is well maintained and fitted out, and has a library, computer room and most of the modern teaching aids.

Memories from the new Burncourt school

Patsy McGrath, Scart

FLASHBACKS TO THE SIXTIES

> Missing out on the excitement and buzz – and the money – of Confirmation Day, as I had already been confirmed at home when I was ill. Serving my first Mass – alone – to Fr Fitzgerald, as the senior server who shall remain nameless, did not turn up and receiving half an orange afterwards from Mrs. Morrissey. Question posed by principal to the class; What is the first thing that happens to a stone when you throw it into a bucket of water? It gets wet sir. Perfect answer by Brian Casey. Got my first smell of 'Wintergreen' in the old school as the Burncourt team got ready to play Kilbehenny in a replayed football tournament final in Eddie Conway's field. The player rubbing the liniment was Francis Meehan. Doing headlines to practice writing with my right hand, for Miss Russell, to prevent me becoming a citeóg [a left-handed person]. Doing woodwork with Mrs. Walsh while the girls did sewing. Having great games of football on Friday nights at Cahills, Coolagarranroe with Cahills, O'Briens, Slatterys, Caseys and Vaughans.

Mary Landers (née Fitzgerald), Cullineagh

I was driven to school on my first morning by my brother Tom, on the carrier of his bicycle. I can still remember the excitement, my new frock and boots, schoolbag, copy and pencil and one penny from my father to spend in Mrs. Duggan's Shop [about 3c today]. Up close the school seemed so big, high windows, higher ceilings; the excitement turning to fear and tears. Miss Coughlan was my first teacher and even though she was only in her early twenties, to a five-year old she was a mature adult who took on the role of mother between nine and three.

My fondest memories are those very early years in Miss Coughlan's class. She taught us the core subjects plus cooking, knitting, Irish dancing and the tin whistle. I especially remember those early cooking classes when on one occasion I shared First Prize with my sister Betty. Our culinary delight was pancakes. The prize was really won by default because we had not brought enough milk and as a result our pancakes were the most firm. I had first choice of a prize; a book or a jigsaw puzzle of 'The Monkeys', a band of the Sixties. I chose the puzzle, still a much treasured possession. I still have it with the pieces intact over forty years later. Students of today would be horrified to learn that cooking was done over a solid fuel cooker in the classroom, almost Stone Age by today's standards. At the time open fires heated the class rooms, fires that were mostly cleaned out, lit and fuelled by the pupils and on cold winter's days, the class was taught around the fire; Health and Safety was unheard of in those far-off days.

Knitting was a popular subject for girls at primary level. In later years, I remember having the pleasure of knitting a jumper, scarf, a vest and vivid memories of knitting socks and the dreaded 'turning the heel'. This took a major effort and time and to cap it all, they were never worn!

Playground activities will always hold pleasant memories, for it was there that friendships were forged. Playtime for girls was playing ballgames against the school wall and skipping in the school yard. I could have skipped for Ireland and I thought I was so good! Thirty years later I won a prize at a Macra Field Evening in Mitchelstown for my skipping ability, proof that education is not wasted. We were fit children because apart from skipping, we walked to and from school, six miles in all. My constant walking companions were my brother Jimmy, Rita and Andrew English and Margaret Maher.

In the Sixties, apartheid was a way of life in many parts of the world. Burncourt School was no different and segregation was very much part of the playground. Boys were segregated from girls at playtime; the only contact

I remember was when it snowed. Snowballs were hurled from side to side as the boys were the enemy, but we had great fun.

Fifty years ago, Burncourt School had a much prized possession, the envy of many a rural school and of the homes of most of the pupils, which today would be considered almost primitive not to have at least two or three in most homes – a flush toilet!

In those days of large families, it was not unusual to have brothers and sisters in the same class. In my class of eighteen, one third was brother and sister. Lunches were always taken outside, bottles of milk and the occasional flask, thick cuts of bread sandwiches filled with whatever was in season and often home produced – blackberry or plum jam – no rolls filled from the hot deli counter then.

Memories of those days at school would not be complete without a mention of an integral part of school life when finances allowed and that was a visit to Mrs. Duggan's Shop. There was a high counter and an array of penny bars, Black Jacks and Flash Bars and Flash Bars were my favourite.

Thoughts of later years in school are scarred by the memories of the Bamboo and the Ash, very much part of the educational system of the time. However my memories of Burncourt National School overall are of fun, kindness, enjoyment and of course learning.

Interviews from senior pupils of Burncourt School in 2006

The senior pupils interviewed their parents, relations or neighbours and submitted the results in essay form for inclusion in the book *Burncourt National School*, which was published to commemorate the fiftieth anniversary of the school.

Breda Fox went to school in the 1980s. There were eleven in her family. She got to school by car as did the other children. The subjects she did were English, Irish, Maths and Religion. For lunch everyday she had a ham sandwich. There were nine in her class. Most days she played 'catch' at lunchtime. The teacher was Pat O'Callaghan. She wore a uniform to school. The most exciting thing that happened was the school tour and these were to Killarney. [Laura Smith]

Pat Butler [Ballyhurrow] went to school in 1942. Back then there were 90 children in the school and there were 12 in his class. His subjects were English, Irish, Maths, Geography, History and Religion. For lunch he got a bottle of milk, sandwiches and a bun. They didn't have a lot of games and only played in the yard. He played rounders, hunt and handball. The teachers were Miss English, Mr. Ahern, Mr. O'Callaghan and Mr. Daly. The pupils wore their normal shorts and pants to school and no shoes in the summer. They had nature walks, a day out in a bus to Sunbeam Wolsey and the Wool Factory in Cork. Pat made his First Communion in 1945 and got his confirmation in 1948. In the evening Pat did homework, chores and played. For homework he got spellings and maths. For sports he played football outside. There were no flush toilets in the school. [Emma-Jane Ryan]

James Tobin [Clogheenafisoge] went to school in 1936. There were 30 in his class and 135 in the school. Years ago they had no cars and the children had to walk to school. The subjects they did were Irish, English, Geography and Maths. They used to bring their lunch to school. They played football. The teachers were Miss English, Mrs O' Callaghan and the principal was Mr. O'Callaghan. They had no uniform and wore normal clothes. The children used to fight and argue before school. He got his First Communion on Sunday and his Confirmation was on a Sunday too. They used to do jobs after school. There were two bullies in school. [Sharon Curtin]

John Shaw [Ballysheehan] played mostly catch and soccer in the school yard. For lunch most of them ate sandwiches. The teachers at that time were Mrs. Quirke, Mrs. Moran and Mr. O'Callaghan. There were around twelve in his class and 80 in the school. After school he played soccer. They had great fun on school tours. His favourite subject was Maths. He got driven to school most days. He got his Confirmation in March 1989 and finished Primary School that year. After Burncourt he went to St. Joseph's in Cahir. [Stacey Shaw]

Danny Fitzgerald [Cullenagh] started school in 1966 and finished in 1974. He was one of a family of eight. There were seven girls and one boy in his class. He used to walk to school and home. His subjects were Irish, Maths, English and History. He took bread and jam for lunch. At lunch time they played football. The teacher's name was John Derby. Danny wore short pants, a blue shirt and shoes. Danny had his First Communion when he was in Second Class. He had his Confirmation in 1973 when he was in Fifth Class. They never went on school tours. After school in the evening he worked on the farm until dinner. [James Fitzgerald]

Danny Smith [Burncourt] started school in 1984 at the age of five. There were ten pupils in his class. He got on with the other pupils. Some books he read were long while others were short. He had the same subjects as today. At break time he would eat his sandwiches and play football and soccer. His teachers were Mrs. Quirke, Mrs. Russell and Mr. O'Callaghan. He wore a grey uniform. Nothing very exciting happened while Danny was at school. Danny made his First Holy Communion in 1986 and his Confirmation in 1990. He went to Cork and Co. Clare on his school tours. He played soccer after school. [James O'Sullivan]

John Mulcahy [Glencallaghan] went to Burncourt N.S. between the 1950's and 1960's. He used to walk to school like most children. There were 15 people in his class and 100 in the school. He did English, Irish, Maths, History, Geography, Latin and Poetry. His favourite subject was poetry. His teachers were called Mr. O'Dea, Mr. Derby, Mrs Phelan and Mrs. Breen. His favourite teachers were Mrs. Phelan and Mrs. Breen. They wore no uniform. When they had religion exams, they got a half day. For lunch they had milk, butter or jam sandwiches. They played hurling and hopscotch. He got his First Communion in First Class. They went to Tramore for their school tours and on the way back they stopped in a restaurant in Waterford. After school, he and his friends went robbing orchards. His good memories of school were his friends. He was never bullied as there were not many bullies at that time. [Sarah Mulcahy]

Theresa English went to Burncourt School at four years of age. Her principal's name was John Derby. She walked or cycled to school. For lunch she had bread, jam and milk. Sometimes she had crisps and an apple. She made her First Communion in Burncourt Church as well as her Confirmation. After school she played football and helped her mother with any chores that needed to be done. The subjects she did were English, Irish, Maths, History, Geography and Music. Her favourite subjects were English and Irish. She left school at the age of 12. [Christopher English]

Maureen Creed walked to school every day. Her favourite subject was Maths. They had three breaks; 11.00am, 12.30pm and 2.00pm. At break the children played rounders, catch and hopscotch. Maureen's favourite game was rounders. They had three teachers. Her favourite was the principal Mr. O'Dea. She wore no uniform. She made her First Holy Communion when she was in First Class. For school tours they went to Tramore and after they went to a café in Waterford. She didn't serve as an altar server. [April McClements]

Richie Maher [Moonaloughra] was 11 when he came to Burncourt in 1936. He came from Newcastle. There were 30 in his class and 140 in the school. His favourite subject was Maths and he did it very well at it. He did all the other subjects like Irish, History, etc. Richie like all the other children walked to school. He brought bread and jam for his lunch and played rounders at lunch. They got one break per day. There were three teachers in the school and his favourite was Mr. O'Callaghan. The people who visited the school were usually priests or nuns. Richie got his Confirmation in 1936. He never went on a school tour. [Orna Quirke]

16

Burncourt Church

THE MODERN CHURCH in Burncourt is known as the Church of the Assumption and was opened in 1953 (Fig. 54). It replaced an earlier cruciform-shaped church, which is recorded as St Mary's chapel and which was to the west of the modern church. Both churches stood while the new church was being constructed and the older church was subsequently demolished. The older church was similar to Duhill church and was built around 1812 and renovated in 1874. The surviving fragments of the older church are the headstones, which face towards the site of the old church (Fig. 55), the holy water font donated by

FIG. 54–BURNCOURT CHURCH.

Fig. 55–Burncourt church, headstones in graveyard faced towards site of old church.

Fig. 56–Holy water font from previous church.

FIG. 57–BASE OF HOLY WATER FONT WITH DEDICATION TO JOHANNA DOBBINS (DIED 1929).

the family of Johanna Dobbins (Fig. 56–57), who died in 1929,[9] and some of the candelabras and the bell donated by the family of Adrian Maloney, who died on 8 March while fighting in World War I.

The new church was designed by Boyd-Barrett Architects, Cork, and built by Pyne Brothers, Fermoy. Local labour, including Lar McGrath, was employed during construction. The church has an unusual design in that the interior has concrete columns projecting from the walls and rising from the floor level to the apex of the roof. These are modelled on medieval buildings of cruck construction where the roof was supported by large timbers springing from ground level. The columns in Burncourt church also serve to support the roof. The church originally had altar railings, which were removed in the 1980s to comply with liturgical requirements. A stained-glass window was sponsored by Fr Morrissey, PP and this is on the left side of the altar. When the church was being refurbished in 2002, four new stained-glass windows were inserted and a ramp was added to the entrance.

17

World War I

JOHN REDMOND, leader of the Irish Parliamentary Party, answered Britain's appeal to help the war effort against the Germans and called on the Irish Volunteers to fight in the Great War (1914–1918), or World War I. Redmond's hope was that Britain would reward Irish support and implement Home Rule for Ireland after the war ended. The National Volunteers, who sided with Redmond's appeal, embraced the war effort and by the end of the war an estimated 50,000 Irishmen had lost their lives on the battlefields. South Tipperary volunteers were trained locally in Cahir or Kilworth army barracks before embarking for Europe. Over 150 men enlisted from the Burncourt, Clogheen and Ballyporeen areas, and the thirty names of those who were killed are inscribed on the War Memorial on Castle Street, Cahir. British troops moved to France in August 1914 to halt the German advance into France and Belgium. The war was fought from trenches across what was known as the 'Western Front' in Flanders (west Belgium) and the Somme (northern France). This trench warfare lasted until 1918 and was where the majority of volunteers from Burncourt, Clogheen and Ballyporeen lost their lives. Offensives along the Western Front in the spring of 1915 ended in failure and many local men from the area were killed. Gas was used extensively as a weapon by the Germans in the Second Battle of Ypres, Flanders, resulting in many deaths, including privates William O'Brien and Michael Riordan from Clogheen. Most casualties, however, were in the Somme in 1916 and in the Battle of Passchendaele in 1917. The Germans launched a massive offensive on the Western Front in March 1918 and attempted to break the deadlock, but as the year passed the Allies gained victory and an armistice was signed in November 1918.

Burncourt volunteers

Adrian Maloney

Adrian and his sister Marjorie moved to Burncourt and went to the national school. Their names are recorded in the roll book. He was the son of William Joseph and Frances Maloney, Old Shanbally. Adrian enlisted in 1916 and was posted to the Western Front in February 1917. Adrian served in the Royal Naval Volunteer Reserve, where he was affectionately known to his fellow officers as 'Mick'. The Royal Naval Volunteer Reserve was an infantry unit and Adrian was an intelligence and sniping officer. While home on leave in early 1918, he attended a Red Cross ball in Clonmel. A few weeks later, on 8 March 1918, 20-year-old Sub-Lieutenant Adrian Maloney, from Old Shanbally, Burncourt, was killed by a shell splinter in the area close to the northern French town of Cambrai. He was buried in the village of Ribécourt in France (Fig. 58). His sister Marjorie received a letter from a fellow officer to sympathise and explain that Adrian was killed instantly. His family donated a bell and candelabras to Burncourt church in his memory (Figs 59–60).

FIG. 58–ADRIAN MALONEY'S GRAVE IN RIBÉCOURT. *COURTESY PAUL BUCKLEY*

William Anderson

William was born in Scotland and as a child moved to Rehill Wood with his parents, William and Jane, and brother, Alexander. His family were Scottish Presbyterians who came to work on the Cahir estate, then owned by Lady Margaret Charteris. Rehill Wood was part of the estate and William's father was employed as a gamekeeper in the early 1900s. The young William was employed as a forester in Rehill Wood and his brother as a gardener. Private William Anderson of the Royal Fusiliers was killed in action on 27 July 1916 in the Battle of Delville Wood in the Battle of the Somme. He was 21 years old and his body was never recovered.

FIG. 59–CANDELABRA DONATED TO BURNCOURT CHURCH BY ADRIAN MALONEY'S FAMILY.

FIG. 60–BASE OF CANDELABRA WITH DEDICATION TO ADRIAN MALONEY.

Volunteers from the surrounding districts

Charles Moulson, Clogheen

Charles Moulson was killed in action at the Battle of Ypres on the Western Front in Flanders in November 1914. Moulson was a former soldier from England who married and settled in Barrack Hill, Clogheen, where he worked as a postman. His military knowledge saw him training the Clogheen Irish Volunteers in 1914. As a former soldier he was called to military service at the outbreak of World War I and served with a cavalry regiment. He was awarded the Distinguished Conduct Medal for an act of bravery whilst in action. A memorial plaque was unveiled on Barrack Hill, Clogheen, to commemorate his two sons, Con and George, who both played for the Irish senior international football team. Charles Moulson has no known grave.

James Hogan, Clogheen

Private James Hogan was killed on 9 October 1917 at the Battle of Passchendaele in Flanders, Belgium. He has no known grave.

David Condon, Skeheenarinky

David Condon was born in 1894, a son of Michael and Johanna Condon (née Fitzgerald) from Skeheenarinky, and brother to John, James, Kate, Patrick, Johanna, and Mary Anne. David was a pupil in Skeheenarinky National School from 1899 – 1907. The 1911 Census shows he was living and working with the Williams family on their farm at Coolaprevane, Ballyporeen. David joined his brother James in Wales around 1914. Both men enlisted in the British Army at Caerphilly and Private David Condon is recorded as being in the 1st Battalion, Irish Guards. David gave his Irish address as 'Kilbehenny'. At the end of July 1916, the battalion moved to the Somme.

On the night of the 14 March 1917, David Condon met his brother James at base camp and, perhaps because of some premonition, gave him a photo for a young lady back home in Ireland. On 15 March 1917, the Irish Guards went forward and Private David Condon of Kiltankin was killed in action. He is buried at Sailly-Saillisel British Cemetery in Somme.

Others from the area killed in action

Maurice Walsh: Carrigavisteale, Ballyporeen. West Riding Regiment. Age 23.
William O'Riordan: Ballyporeen. Royal Dublin Fusiliers. Age 17.

18

Kit Conway

A MEMORIAL to Kit Conway was unveiled in Burncourt in June 2005 (Fig. 61) to mark his life as a Republican who fought in the Spanish Civil War. Kit Conway also fought in the War of Independence (1919–21), was part of the local D Company of the 3rd Tipperary Brigade and later joined the No 2 Flying Column under the direction of Seán Hogan. He is, however, best known for his activity in Spain during the Spanish Civil War (1936–39) where he fought fearlessly on the Republican side and was killed at the Battle of Jarama on 12 February 1937. The Christy Moore song 'Viva La Quinta Brigada' paid tribute to the Irishmen who fought against Franco and fascism:

FIG. 61–UNVEILING OF KIT CONWAY MEMORIAL, BURNCOURT 2005.

They came to stand beside the Spanish people
To try and stem the rising fascist tide
Franco's allies were the powerful and wealthy
Frank Ryan's men came from the other side …
This song is a tribute to Frank Ryan, Kit Conway and Dinny Coady too …

The early life of Kit Conway was recalled in an article entitled 'From Tipperary to Jarama … The Story of Kit Conway', by Seán Ua Cearnaigh for the *Irish Democrat* (1987). The story was augmented by Karol De Falco in *Daughters of Dún Iascaigh* (2018). Kit Conway's mother, Ellen Conway, who was unmarried and from Cahir, gave birth to a son named John in 1896 in the Clogheen Workhouse. A second son named Christopher was also born in the workhouse in 1899. Christopher was recorded in the pupil register of Skeheenarinky National School as being enrolled in 1908; the details of his home circumstances are given as living with a farmer and his family in Coolagarranroe. His mother Ellen worked as a farm servant for the Sheely family and Christopher worked as a farm hand in the English household. Seán Ua Cearnaigh details how Christopher worked for the English family from the age of 14. His name is a bit of a mystery, and he was known locally as 'Christy'; the name 'Kit' was taken by him when he moved to Dublin in around 1922. Seán Ua Cearnaigh gives details of Kit Conway's early life, recounting that he was always a republican, although he joined the British Army in 1915 to fight in World War I. Kit soon regretted his decision and, while training in Kilworth Camp, feigned insanity and was discharged.

Kit Conway joined the 3rd Tipperary Brigade and was described by Seán Ua Cearnaigh as 'an excellent soldier and a born leader of men'. A statement[10] given by Lieutenant Colonel Thomas Ryan, 3rd Tipperary Brigade on IRA activity in the years 1914–21 documents that the brigade commanders were initially suspicious of Chris (Kit) Conway, as he was a former British soldier and was possibly a spy. Ryan established that Kit Conway had 'deserted from a number of regiments in the British Army during the war, not because he was afraid to fight but because he felt unwilling to fight for England, though he had been driven by economic pressure to join the British Army in the first place'. As a test of Kit Conway's loyalty, the IRA company commander brought Conway on an attack on the RIC barracks at Ballyporeen. Ryan continues with the story as follows:

> He was posted in the most dangerous position during the attack where we
> kept him under observation, with a view to shooting him at once if he

showed any sign of treachery in his behaviour. Instead, to our surprise, he showed himself fearless and determined in the course of the attack and demonstrated to those of us who watched him how a man should behave under fire. From that night onwards, he became the white-haired boy and was taken into the Column without having taken the Volunteer oath.

Kit Conway became the main instructor in drill and weapons, as he had previous training with the British Army. He is mentioned in a military statement by Maurice McGrath, who detailed the War of Independence. Kit was involved in the Garrymore ambush and on an attack on British soldiers in Kilmannagh, Co. Kilkenny, when the flying column joined with Kilkenny columns.

Kit Conway moved to Dublin after the Civil War and became known as 'Kit Ryan' because he had fought on the anti-Treaty side in the final year of the Civil War and was wanted by the Free State government. He reverted to the name Kit Conway when danger had passed. Kit Conway joined the Irish Brigade under Frank Ryan and went to Spain to fight Franco's fascists. Kit Conway was killed at the Battle of Jarama, near Madrid. Conway's life was one of republicanism and fighting for the causes he believed in.

A version of 'The Galtee Mountain Boy' by Manus O'Riordan includes the lines:

Despite the brave 15th Brigade, Kit Conway to the fore.
Outside Madrid 10,000 killed in Jarama's vale of tears.
In that war's hell Kit Conway felt that Spain might yet be free.
And with freedom Spain a gravestone raised, thanks gave in '94,
Where thousands lay with Kit Conway, far away from Galteemore.
In the year '05, Kit's name to inscribe, 'twas to Burncourt that we came,
Tipperary's fighting story to honour and proclaim!
With his comrades from the War in Spain, Mick O'Riordan and Bob Doyle,
A plaque unveiled, Kit Conway praised, here's to freedom's Galtee Boys!

19

War of Independence

THE VOLUNTEERS were formed in 1914 but after the outbreak of World War I, the Volunteers split into two groups: the National Volunteers, who supported John Redmond's call to join with the British Army in defence of small nations against the might of the German Empire; and the Irish Volunteers, who opposed Redmond and continued to fight against Britain for Irish independence.

The Volunteer network in the Burncourt, Skeheenarinky, Ballylooby and Ballyporeen areas was organised around 1914. The Volunteers in the Burncourt area were part of the 3rd Tipperary Brigade and under the overall command of Seamus Robinson. The areas were divided into battalions and within them there were local companies. The 393 men of 6th Battalion were under the direction of Seán Treacy, who visited the area to organise Volunteer units; Ned McGrath of Cahir became battalion commander. Thomas Ryan of Tubbrid, who provided a statement to the Bureau of Military History, stated that he became acting commanding officer when McGrath was arrested and interned in Wormwood Scrubs. The districts included in the 6th Battalion were Burncourt, Skeheenarinky, Ballyporeen, Rehill, Tincurry, Garrymore, Graigue and Ballybacon (Marnane, 2018). Maurice McGrath's military statement provided an account of their activity and records that there were thirty men in the Burncourt Volunteers, who were G Company. The following men were listed:

Company Captain: John Casey, Boolakennedy
1st Lieutenant: Thomas Tobin, Glengar
2nd Lieutenant: William Cleary, Glengar
Adjutant: Tim Mulcahy, Crannagh
Lt. Dispatcher: John Casey, Boolakennedy
Lt. Engineer: P. Casey, Boolakennedy

D Company of Skeheenarinky also included men from Burncourt; the following were listed:

Company Captain: J.J. Kearney, Coolagarranroe
1st Lieutenant: Ned Mulcahy, the Caves
Adjutant: Patrick Fox, Coolagarranroe
Quartermaster: Maurice McGrath and D. Fitzgerald

There is no complete list[11] of who was in each company; it would have been foolhardy to compile a list and a disaster if it fell into the hands of security forces. Other names mentioned by Maurice McGrath in his military statement include Jack Butler, Jack Creed, Jim Mulcahy, Denis Lonergan (The Sniper), Bill Mulcahy (the caves), Bill Cleary, Thomas O'Gorman, James Regan, Gabriel McGrath and Martin Lyons; Patrick O'Gorman and Michael Lyons joined the flying column in 1921. Thomas Ryan's military statement lists himself, Jack Butler, Millgrove; Maurice McGrath, Burncourt; Denis Lonergan (The Sniper) and Jack Nagle.

The opening shots of the War of Independence were fired at Soloheadbeg, near Tipperary Town, on 19 January 1919. A delivery of gelignite en route to the local quarry, escorted by RIC personnel, was attacked by a contingent of eight men from the 3rd Tipperary Brigade, led by Seamus Robinson, Commanding Officer and aided by Seán Treacy, Dan Breen, Tadhg Crowe, Seán Hogan and three others. Two RIC officers, Constables O'Donnell and O'Connell, were shot dead and the raiding party split up to make their escape. Treacy, Breen and Hogan headed south and made their way to the Galtee Mountains. The snow was on the mountain and this made the crossing treacherous; Seán Treacy fell down a twenty-foot ravine during the ill-advised attempt to escape across Galtymore (Marnane, 2018). The trio decided to go to Cahir, where they sheltered in Mrs Marian (May) Tobin's house in Tincurry and then headed to Tom O'Gorman's, who lived beside Burncourt Castle. From there they were driven by Jack Tobin to Mitchelstown and made their way to Newcastle West, Co. Limerick.

There was a national shortage of arms and ammunition for the Volunteers, including in Co. Tipperary. Arms were procured by raiding RIC barracks, stealing guns from 'big houses' and buying them from ex-British Army personnel who returned to Ireland after World War I. General headquarters in Dublin dispatched some revolvers, ammunition and bandoliers to the Volunteers in the Cahir area in 1920. These were hidden in egg cases and came into Cahir Railway Station. Pat McGrath, whose family owned a shop and pub in Burncourt, exported eggs; he collected the 'empty' egg cases that were used to conceal weapons. A British spy at Cahir Railway Station noticed the activity and informed the authorities. In May 1920, McGrath's business in Burncourt was raided by the military (Black and Tans) and the premises was searched. Bayonets were run through the egg cases but nothing was found. A week later an armoured car took up position at the front door at 8.30 p.m. and a military cycling corps arrived. The house was again searched but nothing was found. The cycling corps withdrew to Rehill Barracks but the armoured car stayed until 6 a.m. Two military men were also posted in the kitchen.

The McGraths refused to sell goods to the eight RIC men stationed at Rehill. Account books from the business were seized by the RIC and the police went over the counter and took what they wanted. The goods were, however, paid for. Raids by the RIC, often accompanied by the military on McGrath's pub and shop, became frequent.

About twenty soldiers were sent to Rehill Barracks to reinforce the police presence. They were billeted in a large tent beside the barracks and patrolled the roads from Cahir to Burncourt. One night the soldiers got out of hand and refused to be bullied by the RIC sergeant. Shots were fired, one soldier was killed and some of the RIC were badly wounded. The barracks was then evacuated and the RIC and soldiers were sent to Cahir and elsewhere. Military patrols continued, however, and raids on houses became frequent. The Burncourt Volunteers (G Company), captained by John Casey and aided by D Company from Skeheenarinky, demolished the Rehill Barracks one night and only narrowly escaped through the fields from a fifty-strong military cycling patrol.

A number of Volunteers from the Burncourt area were arrested and interned. These included Tom O'Gorman, Jack Creed, Denis McGrath, Michael Walsh and Jim Slattery. An autograph book belonging to Maureen Creed, which includes sketches, confirms that some of these men were interned in Ballykinler, Co. Down (Figs 62–63). Jack Creed was initially interned on Spike Island near Cobh and then transported in HMS *Heather* to Ballykinler, Co. Down. The ship was a British navy sloop that was built to look like a merchant ship but had concealed weapons. Jack Creed's internment lasted from December 1919 until December 1920. Like many, he would have had a wife and young children.

It appears, from Maurice McGrath's military statement, that Burncourt was a frequent target of military raids. Ryan's bar (now the Old Shanbally Bar) was owned by Cornelius Ryan and frequented by Lieutenant Gaffney, based in the Cahir military barracks, and Lieutenant Jones from the Clogheen barracks. These men and their troops were known as 'The Murder Gang'. Maurice McGrath wrote that while the army officers were being entertained – presumably drinking in the pub – McGrath's bar was raided and the customers were searched

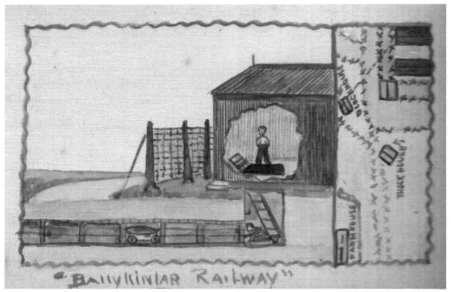

FIG. 62–SKETCH OF BALLYKINLAR INTERNMENT CAMP. *COURTESY MAUREEN CREED*

FIG. 63–SKETCH OF BALLYKINLAR INTERNMENT CAMP. *COURTESY MAUREEN CREED*

and intimidated. Maurice McGrath records in his military statement that the Volunteers raided Ryan's bar and shop in search of guns but did not locate any. The morning after the Volunteer raid on Ryan's bar, a notice was posted on the church wall warning all Sinn Féiners of the serious consequences of interfering with loyal people. The notice was signed 'Anti-Sinn Féin League'. Ned Mulcahy of the caves, who was in D Company (Skeheenarinky), was on his way home for dinner after work at Burncourt Creamery when he called on Maurice McGrath. Both went down to read the notice. McGrath tore it down, went across the road and confronted Ryan, warning him to be careful in the future.

On 20 October 1919 the Murder Gang (possibly led by Gaffney and Jones) came to Burncourt from Ballyporeen. They raided Fox's of Killavenoge and burned the hay barn. Pat Fox was out and only his parents were at home. At midnight the army went to Pat McGrath's home in Skeheenarinky, where they broke all the windows, wrecked and looted the house, and turned his wife and children and his aged parents out in the cold. This contingent came to Burncourt village at 1 a.m. Pat and Maurice McGrath and their nephew Jimmy were on the premises. The soldiers battered the front door with rifle butts. Maurice looked out the upstairs window and was ordered to open the door. His description goes on to say that 'in rushed in a dozen or so masked savages'. The soldiers shot the lock off the bar door and began what Maurice described as a 'drinking orgy'. The captain shoved Maurice upstairs into a bedroom and pulled Pat McGrath from his bed. Pat's trousers were pulled from him. There was £120 in a pocket, from the bar takings and the sale of a horse, but it appears this wasn't taken. The army captain ordered both Maurice and Pat to their knees, told them they had five minutes to live and started counting down the minutes. Pat and Maurice fully expected to be shot. Shots were then fired into the bedroom ceiling. The McGrath brothers were then taken out and flogged with belts until 3 a.m. Both men fell into unconsciousness. Mrs O'Gorman of Burncourt Castle heard the shots and shouting, and sent the Volunteers Jim Mulcahy and Jack Tobin to help. The Murder Gang had left at this stage. Jim Mulcahy and Jack Tobin arrived from across the fields and took the McGrath brothers into their house. They reported back to Mrs O'Gorman, who sent a pony and trap to bring the McGraths to Skeheenarinky; she was unaware that their home at Cahergal had been wrecked. Maurice stayed in Burncourt and Pat went to Skeheenarinky. Dr Walsh was called and he brought Pat to Clogheen Hospital, where he spent six weeks under military guard, as the intention was to arrest him. Sister Austin, from the hospital, was a cousin of Mrs O'Gorman; she and Dinny O'Callaghan, the hospital porter, got Pat over the wall and he escaped to Mitchelstown. Pat suffered from the beatings for the rest of his short life.

Ned Mulcahy, from the caves, called to McGrath's the day after the raid and was just inside the door when Lieutenants Gaffney and Jones arrived with an escort. The officers tried to question Maurice McGrath but Ned intervened and said he was unwell after the beating. The lieutenants were unaware that Ned Mulcahy was 1st Lieutenant of the Volunteer D Company in Skeheenarinky. Once the army left, Ned and some friends arranged for Maurice McGrath to go

FIG. 64–SOME MEMBERS OF BURNCOURT FLYING COLUMN. FROM LEFT TO RIGHT: -?-, DINNY (THE SNIPER) LONERGAN, JACKIE (JOHN) TOBIN, MAURICE MCGRATH.

to a safe house on the Galtees, where he recovered after eight days.

The constant British Army raids led to the formation of the flying columns under the direction of Seán Hogan, and these reduced the number of raids on Volunteer homes, where people were beaten, shot at and arrested. The flying columns around Burncourt were organised in December 1920. Maurice McGrath became Adjutant of No 2 Flying Column. The flying column members in the Burncourt area (Fig. 64) were listed by Maurice McGrath as follows:

D Company: Ned Mulcahy [caves], Denis Lonergan [The Sniper], Davy Fitzgerald. Chris Conway [Kit Conway] was the company trainer.
C Company: Tommy Ryan (Ballylooby), Tom Mullaney.
F Company: Dave Maher, Bill Mulcahy, Bill Keating, Frank Pyne, Davy Quirke, Bill O'Brien.

The flying columns were mobile, making use of hit-and-run tactics, and the units were small, easily hidden in safe houses, and began guerrilla warfare with proactive attacks on the British military forces. The flying columns attacked RIC barracks to try and procure guns and ammunition. The Cahir–Mitchelstown road was constantly used by the British military and was a target for No 2 Flying Column. Felling trees and trenching across the road made the military easier targets, as these roadblocks stopped the convoys. Bridges at Glengarra and

Brackbawn were destroyed. The military used planks to cross the holes made in the roads, or rounded up locals working in the fields to fill them in. The local Volunteers remained active and continued with harassing the military. Once the roads were repaired by the British, the local Volunteers dug trenches across them again.

The British military forces were a constant presence in the Burncourt area. Maurice McGrath records that, towards the end of May 1921, an advance party of the flying column waited near the ball alley at Kilcoran in order to attack a military convoy, but the convoy, escorting General Strickland to Cork, comprised ninety-six vehicles. The planned attack had to be aborted as the flying column was vastly outnumbered. The column members were hidden in the ditch and were fired on, but none were injured. At the same time, a contingent of seventy lancers from Cahir Military Barracks travelled what was known as 'the old Cahir road' and arrived in Burncourt, and then went up to the Mitchelstown–Cahir road. Thomas Ryan also records that after an abortive strike on the railway line at Donohill, the flying column crossed the Galtees and had reached Rehill Wood when two hundred lorries carrying British troops passed by on their way to Cork. The soldiers were in the habit of firing pot-shots into the wood, and the column narrowly missed being shot. The military activity around Burncourt must have been very unsettling for the people in the area, as the military were at best intimidating but also prone to attacking houses and residents.

Maurice McGrath records how the D Company Flying Column shot at an RIC patrol, killing one and badly wounding another at Cahill's Cross. This may have been around March 1921. There was also an account of the Garrymore ambush at Hyland's Cross on 23 April 1921. The local flying column, under the command of Dinny Lacey, attacked a convoy of British lorries, and in that incident the lorries were burnt, one soldier was killed and two later died from their wounds (Hallinan, 1993). The remaining soldiers were disarmed and the flying column fled to the Galtees under the command of the Burncourt captain, John Casey. The column went by Rehill Wood and were in Casey's house, having just crossed the Burncourt–Ballylooby road, when five lorries full of British soldiers passed on the road going to Burncourt. Other lorries carrying British troops passed along the Cahir–Mitchelstown road to the north. Captain Casey and John and Thomas Tobin acted as scouts and got the column to safe houses.

The capture and execution of District Inspector Gilbert Potter
Just before Dinny Lacey and his column left for Newcastle after the Garrymore ambush, District Inspector (DI) Potter, who was based in Cahir, arrived at the ambush site. District Inspector Potter was a high-ranking RIC official. The

FIG. 65–DI POTTER'S GRAVESTONE.

Volunteers were almost dispersed after the Garrymore ambush when DI Potter, who was dressed as a civilian, stopped his car at the site of the burnt-out lorries. A Volunteer named Downey asked DI Potter for a light for his pipe and saw a revolver on the car seat. Potter was arrested by Downey and handed over to the flying column. After his capture, Potter was taken to the Newcastle area and kept in a 'safe-house' for one night. British troops were searching for Potter and he was moved on to the Nire Valley the next day (Hallinan, 1993). The IRA HQ in Dublin offered to exchange Potter for Volunteer Thomas Traynor, who was under death sentence in Dublin. Traynor was hanged and Potter was then shot in Clonea Power.

Potter was a family man and had four children under seven. He wrote to his wife Lily on 24 April while being held prisoner, saying he was being treated well and apologising for the distress caused to her by his kidnapping (Hallinan, 1993). Another letter on 27 April said he hoped that his kidnappers would pity his wife 'who is Irish as I am also'. Potter was buried in what is known as the 'Protestant Graveyard' outside Cahir (Fig. 65).

As a reprisal for DI Potter's death, houses were blown up by the Tans. In Burncourt, the houses were Tom O'Gorman's of Burncourt Castle and Mulcahy's of the caves. Other houses included Mrs Tobin's of Tincurry House, James Slattery's of Kilbeg and McCarthy's of Drumlummin.

Ballygiblin Roundup

A major operation by the British military forces was the 'Ballygiblin Roundup'. The precise date is unclear but it was after the capture of DI Potter, possibly May 1921. It almost annihilated the local flying column, who were billeted in various nearby houses around Kiltankin and Ballygiblin. Seán Hogan was the captain and led a column of thirty men. British forces from Mitchelstown, Kilworth Camp, Moorepark and Fermoy and forces from Tipperary, Clonmel, Cahir and Clogheen numbered 3,000 troops and 100 horsemen. The roundup began at 4 a.m. and every house, drain and boreen was searched by small contingents of foot soldiers and horsemen. The army presence was noticed by farmers going to the creamery and they tipped off the flying column members that were spread out in various safe houses; these houses were searched, but at that stage the flying column members had left. When the British troops were searching houses, they were offered tea – this was a delaying tactic by the locals which enabled the flying column men to escape.

Seán Hogan decided to lead the men towards Mitchelstown; Maurice McGrath and Dave Moher, who were locals, acted as guides. The column crossed the Furrough (Furrow) Bog and was warned by Ms O'Hanrahan, the teacher at Ballygiblin National School, that the entire area south of Ballygiblin was occupied by troops. The column crossed the road at Ballygiblin and the Tans, who were holding up farmers going to the creamery, failed to spot them. They headed into Molan's yard where Mr Molan told them to hide in a dyke in a field behind the house. The dyke was sheltered from view by sallies at the front and furze on top of a high boundary fence. Soldiers came into the yard and into the field behind the dyke but failed to spot the column. Soldiers on horseback came up behind the column in the dyke, but one horse refused to jump and the contingent headed back to the Ballygiblin–Mitchelstown road. All males in the area from 15 to 70 years were rounded up by the troops and detained. Yet the British forces failed to locate the column. The column sheltering in the dyke heard shots and saw Varey lights (flares) coming from Ballygiblin School, thinking that they would be found; fortunately these signals were for the British troops to retreat – the column was safe. They went north to the Galtees and sheltered in James Regan's house near Galtee Castle.

A large party of troops on horseback descended on the area where men were billeted around Galtee Castle. A quick-thinking Christy (Kit) Conway dashed under one horse and caused a stampede, which allowed himself and Dave Moher to hide their guns and escape. Frank Pyne was captured, but he was unarmed; he claimed he was working in the area and was going to Mrs Fitzgerald's house, as she was alone. Pyne was arrested and sentenced to five years in jail.

The truce came into effect on 11 July 1921 and ended the War of Independence.

20

Ned Tobin: Athlete Supreme

NED TOBIN was born in 1911 in a house just after the metal bridge on the road from Burncourt to Ballylooby. His sporting field was weight throwing. As a boy he practiced the sport by throwing weights over the hay barn in Casey's farm in Glengar. Ned Tobin held world records in throwing the 56lb weight, both in distance and over-the-bar, and was described as 'one of the most durable of all Irish athletes', appearing in competitions for over thirty years.

Ned was 6ft 5in (2m) tall and of slim build. He joined the Gardaí in 1933 at 22 years of age; he was initially stationed in Fingal and then moved to Garristown, where he was promoted to sergeant and was ultimately sergeant in

Fig. 66–Ned Tobin pictured here at the Garda sports in 1936, winning the 56lb over the bar contest at which he set an new national record of 15ft 3½in (Pathé News).

charge of the new recruits training section at Garda Headquarters in the Phoenix Park.

Ned attended the Olympics in Berlin in 1936, but as the International Amateur Athletic Association prohibited all Irish athletes from taking part in international events – and Ned was a member of the Irish National Athletic and Cycling Association – Ned was unable to participate. Ned was an all-round athlete and was also an outstanding hurdler, a sound performer in the shot put and javelin, and the long and triple jumps. During his career he won 34 National Championship medals for weight-throwing, 28 medals for discus, 18 for shot and 11 for hammer. He won five national championships in one afternoon in Thurles in 1939. His world records included one for weight-throwing in Ballina in 1943.

21

Power in the Valley

THE ESB was established by the government in 1927, and rural electrification began with the Shannon Hydro-Electric Scheme in 1929. Initially, electrification was concentrated in urban areas because there was little money in government coffers to extend the process nationwide. There were, however, small-scale electricity suppliers scattered throughout the country, including in Cahir, Newcastle and Clogheen. John Browne of Clogheen supplied electricity before 1927, when he had sixty-eight homes connected; this rose to ninety-one homes by 1945. The Cahir scheme had 137 homes in 1929 and 145 in 1930. These small-scale schemes were acquired by the ESB when rural electrification began. Many large country houses, including Shanbally Castle, also generated electricity for their own use.

Life before electricity was difficult; lighting was by oil lamps, candles or gaslight. The gaslight was run from a gas cylinder via a pipe to the light, and was turned on and off by a chain which opened or closed the gas supply to the mantle. This was the system used in Mountain Lodge up to recent years. After electrification, light was at the turn of a switch. Washing was previously done by hand or with a clothes wringer. Heating was achieved by fires, and these were also used to cook: kettles and pots were hung from a crane over the fire. There are many black kettles and bastables (large cooking pots) discarded around the countryside and now frequently used as flower-pots. There were no fridges, and fresh meat was stored in a 'food-safe', which was a small cupboard with tight-mesh wire on the door. Most meat was salted or smoked and hung in the kitchen or pantry. Electricity also enabled water to be piped into houses, which was a great bonus as water no longer had to be drawn from the river or the well.

The ESB archive confirms that rural electrification began in Burncourt in mid-September 1957 and was completed in February 1958. Nightly demonstrations were given in Burncourt, Clogheen and Ballyporeen on the

FIG. 67–GAS DELIVERY TO MCGRATH'S, BURNCOURT, 1963. *COURTESY BREDA MCGRATH*

benefits of electricity. Goods such as water heaters, pumps, kettles, clothes irons, cookers, Burco Boilers and a single washing machine were sold at the demonstrations in Burncourt. Overall, 223 customers in Burncourt were connected to the ESB supply at a total cost of £1,538.80. There was 42km of high-tension and 25km of low-tension line strung from 715 poles. Locals were hired to dig the pole-holes. D.E. Lynch, from the ESB, was in charge and in a memorandum on the process he noted that one of the difficulties was the amount of water encountered. The poles had to be erected immediately on excavation, as the holes became filled with water. The poles were imported from the Baltics for the nationwide scheme as there was a shortage of suitable poles in Ireland. Individual houses in Burncourt were wired for electricity in the Burncourt area by Davy Whelan of Upper Burncourt. At the time of the electrification, D.E. Lynch noted that Shanbally Castle was famous because of the dispute between those who wanted to retain the castle and the Land Commission, who wanted to level the castle, and that plans were being drawn up to divide the estate. The ESB provided the Land Commission with a layout of the electrical grid so that new houses could be built close to the power lines.

The other major improvement to the households was the arrival of the New World gas cooker in the early 1950s. The local agent for these cookers was

Rodger McGrath, Burncourt (Fig. 67). The gas cooker made cooking much easier and dinners were made without having to light the fire. Gas was used to power some appliances, including clothes irons; the iron was fitted to the gas pot, the gas was lighted to heat the iron and, hey presto – nicely ironed clothes.

22

Miscellaneous

Feis in Burncourt

The Cork Examiner, on Wednesday, 4 August 1904, reported on a Feis-Aeridheacht (Oidheacht) which was held in the grounds of Burncourt Castle 'kindly given by the owner Mr Michael Cashin'. Attendees were from Clogheen, Cahir, Clonmel, Kilbehenny and Newcastle. A stage was erected and Burncourt schoolchildren had a banner in Irish reading '*Ar Erin*'.

In the English language category, Burncourt swept the boards with Ms Bridie English tied for first place in spoken language, May Ryan in second and Nora Galvin in third. Mr M.J. Duhill of Burncourt, who had previously won a prize in Mitchelstown, sang an old Irish song and was loudly applauded.

Mr O'Donoghue of Mitchelstown addressed the gathering in Irish and English and appealed to keep the language alive, as well as traditional games. His plea to have the children learn the Irish language and Irish sports was loudly applauded. The priest, Fr Ormonde, announced the prize winners and thanked the teachers of Burncourt for their assistance.

Whort picking in the 1930s–1940s

Whorts (pronounced hurts), or bilberries, grow in woodland, on mountain sides and in boggy areas; they were picked in the Burncourt area and elsewhere, particularly during the war years, as a food but also as an income supplement. Whorts are similar to but smaller than blueberries and they ripen from June to October (Conry, 2011). The berries were eaten raw, made into pie filling and also exported to Britain, particularly during and just after World War II. The price given to the picker in the 1930s was a half-crown a stone; Michael J. Conry has shown that its export value from 1941–1950 was in the region of £173,660, with peaks in exports in 1941 and 1946. The price paid to the pickers was exceptionally high and can be gauged against the wages of a young farm labourer, who could expect 5*s*. a week. The money from picking whorts was used to supplement the household budget when times were lean during World War II. At this time in Ireland there was very little social welfare and people had to earn a crust wherever they could.

One of the buyers who travelled to the Burncourt area during the 1940s was Stephen Prendergast from Kilsheelan (Conry, 2011). Other buyers in the area included the Grubbs of Castlegrace and the Brownes in Clogheen. In later years, the whorts were bought by Mrs Hickey of Kilcoran. Whorts were plentiful on the southern slopes of the Galtees, from Kilbehenny to Kilcoran. Glengarra Wood was a prime source of whorts, with pickers coming from Burncourt, Skeheenarinky and Ballyporeen, as well as Cahir. People travelled to Mountain Lodge on a donkey and cart and walked out to where the whort bushes were growing. Conry (2011) interviewed locals from Burncourt for his book on whort-picking and was told by Tom Finn of how his mother, Ellen, father, John, and sisters, Peggy, Mary and Bridie, went by pony and trap and he how rode his bicycle. Tom's father was a stonemason and the building trade was very slack during World War II, so he had plenty of time to pick whorts. The price was 12*s*. a stone, but as the season progressed the price rose as high as 30s. Peggy Cleary (née O'Shea) of Glengarra Lodge bought the whorts for Stephen Prendergast; she weighed the whorts and paid what was due.

Community hall and council

The Community Council was formed in Burncourt in 1977. One of the first tasks undertaken was the development of a community centre. With this end in mind, the following group formed: Martin Connolly was the chairman, Mary McGrath was the secretary and the committee members were Pakie Reardon, Seán Creed, Patsy Crotty, Mary English, Ned McGrath, Dan Dowling and Fr Michael Ryan. The former national school was bought from Shanbally estate and renovated, including the building of toilets and a kitchen to the rear. This provided a facility which is still in use today. Through the years, various improvements have been made, but the original task was huge given the limited resources; the community centre is now an important community venue. Fundraising back in 1977 included card games, raffles and a non-stop draw, and the whole community got behind the venture.

Millennium Stone

At the turn of the twenty-first century, much discussion took place on how best to commemorate the event. Coillte Teo planted a Millennium Forest in Glengarra Wood and each tree was allocated to a family. Burncourt Community

Council came up with the idea of having a permanent record of all those who lived in the district at the time; out of this was born the Millennium Stone, which was erected beside the church. The stone costs were covered in part by local donations and partly by the National Millennium Committee. The stone is limestone and was cut and inscribed by Quarrystone Quarries. The shape on top of the stone represents the Galtee Mountains. All the names are inscribed on a seven-sided base (Fig. 68).

FIG. 68–MILLENNIUM STONE.

23

Townland Names in the Vicinity of Burncourt

THE INFORMATION on townlands is from *The Place-Names of Decies*, compiled by Canon Patrick Power in the early 1900s. Townland names, with translations and some other information on place names, are presented below.

Townland names
Townland names and place names are usually descriptive of a topographical feature in a landscape such as 'drom', meaning 'hill', or 'rehill', meaning 'level topped'. Other names can be derived from ownership, like 'Ballysheehan' or 'Sheehan's homestead', or from legendary or historical figures such as Dawson's Table on the Galtee Mountains, or, less frequently, from occupations or trades where the tools of the trade (spade) or products (milk, butter, honey, etc.) may be used as part of a place name. Other names derive from pastimes, like 'Skeheenarinky' from *'rince'* (dancing).

Many townland boundaries reflect ancient territorial divisions that are perhaps as early as prehistoric times. Townlands are themselves grouped into baronies; these again are ancient territories probably belonging to tribal units prior to the Anglo-Norman conquest of Ireland in the late twelfth century. Most townland names are Celtic in origin, and in the Burncourt area many are derived from early Irish and reflect the early centuries after Christ when the area was part of the Decies territory, who controlled the region from the third century. Parishes date from later times, after the Anglo-Norman invasion (1169).

In the seventeenth century an act was passed commanding the use of English instead of Irish in certain cases. This act decreed:

> His Majesty taking notice of the barbarous and uncouth names by which most of the towns and places in this Kingdom of Ireland are called, which … are very troublesome in the use …

The act goes on to decree that:

> For the future how new and proper names more suitable to the English tongue may be inserted … which henceforth be the only names to be used.

By and large the name changes decreed by the act did not take place and many of the townland names remained in use. English names were also usually a direct translation of Irish, and on occasion the names may be incorrect, having lost the original meaning. In the area around Burncourt, most names can be translated directly from the original Irish, as Irish was retained and spoken in this area up to the 1900s; many words are still in use which are directly from Irish, such as cipins (*cipini* or small sticks) or dried dung used for fuel (*bohán*).

Burncourt is in the barony of Iffa and Offa West, which includes fifteen parishes, and Burncourt, with Clogheen, is part of the parish of Shanrahan. Some of the townlands listed below are in the neighbouring parishes of Ballyporeen (the old parish of Templetenny) and Ballylooby (formerly Tubbrid) but are in close proximity to Burncourt.

Shanrahan (Scan Raithean)

Canon Power (1907) describes the parish as follows:

> This is a parish of great extent – stretching from the Co. Waterford boundary line on the south to the ridge of the Galtees to the north. Through it run (east and west) two mountain ranges – the Galtees (Slieve gCrot) and Knockmealdown (Slieve gCua) chains. It is traversed in the same general direction by a couple of small rivers – the Dwag (Dubhaig) and the Tar (An Teara), tributaries of the Suir. Shanrahan is a place of some historic note. The ruined church, dating from a comparatively late period, consists of a nave and chancel joined by a semi-circular arch. At the west end rises a tower of more modern date, and by the south side of the wall, on the outside, is the grave and monument of Rev. Nicholas Sheehy, PP who was hanged and quartered in Clonmel (1766) to the everlasting disgrace of the Cromwellian gentry of South Tipperary. Shanrahan is, or was until recently (early 1900s), an Irish-speaking parish; hence the names are many and interesting. There is a second ruined church (Ballysheehan) within the parish and the sites of two or three primitive oratories.

125

Townlands

The following list gives the modern townland name followed by the Irish name, and thereafter any features in the townland, such as names for roads, hills, fields, etc. This is not a full list of names for fields, or names for other features; the locations of many were unknown to Canon Power.

Ballyhurrow

Baile Uí hUrmhúmha – Ormond's Homestead. Area: 1,118 acres.
Names of places within the townland:
An Stricín – The Little Streak.
Cnoc Fionn – White Hill.
Com a' Dhuine Mhairbh – The Dead Man's Hollow.

Ballysheehan

Baile Uí Shíothcháin – O'Sheehan's Homestead. Area: 244 acres.
The fairs of Ballysheehan were held on 27 August and 4 December.
Names of places within the townland:
Poll Bheití – Betty's Drowning Hole. Named after Betty O'Byrne, who drowned there.

Boolakennedy

Buaile Uí Chinnéide – O'Kennedy's Mountain Milking Place. Area: 1,047 acres.
Names of places within the townland:
Gleann Mór – Great Glen.
Poll an Eara – Hole of the Waterfall.
Cnoc na Ladhaire – Hill of the River Fork.
Móin a' Ghuail – Bog of the Charcoal.
Cnuicín Toiteóige – Little Hill of the Explosion.

Burncourt

Cúirt Dhóighte – Burncourt. Area: 301 acres.
Power writes that the townland owes its name to 'the (late Tudor) castle of the Everards which was destroyed by fire within a few years of its erection, though the limestone walls still stand in an excellent state of preservation'. He also notes that: 'Sir Richard Everard, the builder of the castle and last holder of the barony, played many parts in the stirring times wherein his lot was cast'.

Names of places within the townland:

Mullach na Cille – Ancient Church Summit. The site of this early religious establishment will be found due north – at a distance of two fields – from the church. In the process of quarrying limestone for burning in a kiln close at hand, a greater portion of the cill (church) site has been cut away.

Carriganroe

Carragán Ruadh – Little Red Rock. Area: 337 acres.

Names of places within the townland:

Corragan – No translation.

Carrigmore

Carrig Mhór – Great Rock. Area: 354 acres.

The name derives from a stony outcrop extending for a considerable distance near south-east angle of Shanbally demesne wall.

Names of places within the townland:

Lag a'tSagairt – The Priest's Hollow.

Scairt na Beárnan – Shrubbery of the Gap. A subdivision; formerly an independent townland: Scartinbarnyin Everard Patent.[12]

Clogheen Market

Cloichín a' Mhargaidh – Little Rock of the Market. Area: 320 acres.

The 'Little Rock', upon which the name-giving market was held, is on Pound Lane on the north bank of the Dwag. Old fair dates were 6 April, Whit Monday, 28 October and 12 December.

Names of places within the townland:

Clashleigh (Clair Laith) – Grey Trench.

Clashaphooka (Clair a' Phúca) – The Pooka's Trench.

Crannagh

Crannach – Wooden Stockade. Area: 144 acres.

Names of places within the townland:

Cranoghton (or Cronaghane or Crenaghtewnw) – No translation.

Abhainn Bheag – Little River. The name refers to the stream that flows along the south boundary and enters the Tar at Garryroe.

Cullenagh

Cuileannach – Holly Abounding.

One particular field in this area is called Páirc a'Cuilinn; this may have given the townland its name. The townland is immense in size (it extends from north of the old Cork–Dublin Road [N8] to south of the Ballyporeen Road from Coakley's Cross, and is recorded on the Ordnance Survey maps as Cullenagh North and South).

Names of places within the townland:

Galtybeg (Gaibhlte Beaga) – Mountain Peaks. The mountain peak is the second highest on the Galtee Mountains and was the northern boundary of the ancient territory of the Decies. Height: 2,586ft. The name appears as 'Galtiebegge' in the Everard Patent.

O'Loughnan's Castle (Caisleán Lachtnáin). This is a natural rock outcrop which looks like a castle from a distance; local tradition identifies O'Loughnan as an outlaw.

Greenane (Grianán) – Sunny Place. Peak on the Galtee Mountains; Height 2,624ft.

Cúil Bhán – White Corner.

Log Riabhach – Grey Hollow.

Cnoc Riabhach – Grey Hill.

Páirc na mBan – The Women's Field.

Ladhar Ruadh, Ladar Mhór and Ladar Bheag – Red River-Fork, Great River-Fork and Little River-Fork, respectively.

Cnoc na gCapall – Horses Hill. This appears to be an independent ploughland in Everard's Patent.

Macha Mhurchaidh – Morgan's (or Murrogh's) Milking Yard.

Com Laoigh – Hollow of the Calf.

Beárna Bhán – White Gap.

Macha Cloiche – Stony Milking Yard.

Slior na Carraige – Border of the Rock.

Cnoc Fiaidh – Deer Hill.

Cnoc a' Tuair – Hill of the Cattle Field.

Coolantallagh

Cúil an Teallaigh – Corner of the Seizure (of land, stock, etc.).

Names of places within the townland:

Cúil – Corner. A subdivision.

Móin na Ruicí – Bog of the Wrinkles.

Áth Fionnóige – Scaldcrow Ford. It is on the boundary with Coolagarranroe.

Garrandillon

Garrán Diolúin – Dillon's Grove. Area: 477 acres.

Shanbally Castle, the former residence of Lord Lismore stood in this townland.

Glencallaghan

Gleann Uí Cheallacháin – O'Callaghan's Glen. Area: 131 acres.

Glengarra

Gleann Garra – Garra's Glen. Area 1,029 acres.

O'Donovan (the compiler of Ordnance Survey letters) identifies 'Garra' (a Fianna warrior) as the son of Morna.

Names of places within the townland:

Macha na Ladhaire – Milking Place of the River Fork

Hopkinsrea

Cuileannach – Holly Abounding. Area: 460 acres.

Inchnamuck

Inre na Muc – Holm (little island in a river) of the Pigs. Area: 274 acres.

Killavenoge

Cill a'Bhionóg – Meaning uncertain. Area: 43 acres.

O'Donovan suggests this could be translated as 'Winoc's Church'. Winnocus was a Breton; the Feast of St Winnocus is traditionally on 5 November. The name may also stem from Unniue whose feast is on 29 August. The name (Killavenoge) may also be translated as 'Cill Domhnóc'.

Names of places within the townland:

Bóithrín a' Mhinirtéir – The Minister's Little Road.

Kilbeg

Coill Bheag – Little Wood. Area: 230 acres.

Names of places within the townland:

Tobar Lóid – Lloyd's Well. So called because of a mid-eighteenth-century Bishop of Waterford – Sylvester Llyod, OFM (1739–50) – who blessed it.

Knockarum

Cnoc Atharum – Meaning uncertain.

The name may be a corruption of Eachdhroma – Ridge of the Horses.

Monaloughra

Móin na Luachra – Bog of the Rushes. Area: 156 acres.

Raheenroe

Ráithín Ruadh – Little Red Rath. Area: 185 acres.

A large motte-like rath (ringfort), still entire.

Rehill

Réidh-Coill – Level Topped (or open) Wood. Area: 789 acres.

A portion of this ancient forest survived until quite recently (the early 1900s). Geoffrey Keating, the historian, hid for a time in the recesses of this wood according to a local story. Part of the townland is in Tubbrid Parish.

Places within the townland:

Graveyard. This is a primitive church site. A field close at hand is called Carraigín an Lubhair ('Little Rock of the Yew Tree'), while the church itself is called Cill an Lubhair.

Rehill Wood. Site of Rehill Castle. Also known as 'Roghill Castle'; the castle was held by some Ulster footmen and was captured without resistance by Cromwell, on 1 February 1649.

Glennyreea River (Gleann Aimhréidh) – Crooked (or uneven) Glen.

Scart

Scairt – Thicket. Area 367 acres.

An ancient road ('Bóthar na Miorán' or 'Bóthar na Miorcán') ran east and west through this townland; its route on the east side of the demesne is at a place still marked by gate piers; on the west side, it was a few perches north of Scartnabearna crossroads.

Names of places within the townland:

An seana shéipéal – The old chapel. This is the site of a church from the Penal times – Power records that Fr Sheehy ministered in this church.

Tobar na Cárca – Easter Well. A holy well that is still resorted to. The reputation for sanctity here does not appear to be of an ancient date; it probably arose from the well's propinquity to the church. The well is sometimes called Tobar Mullaigh Chéarta – 'Well of the Mount of Suffering' (Calvary).

Páirc na bPilibíní – Field of the Plover.

Shanbally

Seana Bhaile – Old Village. Area: 371 acres.

On this townland are the graveyard and ruined church commonly called

Ballysheehan. The church is of considerable size and the cemetery contains a few monuments and inscriptions of age and interest.

Toor Mór and Toor Beag
Tuar – Cattle Field (Great and Small). Area: 623 acres.

Templetenny (Teampall Tuinne)
Powers wrote that 'like Shanrahan, Templetenny is a parish of great extent and embraces a large area of mountainous lanscape. The townlands are, as a rule, very large and as Irish is generally understood, sub-denominations (local names) are numerous'. The parish name, Teampall Tuinne, translates as 'Church of the Marsh', which is not shared with a townland; it is evidently derived from the church's position on an island of dry land in what must have been a bog previous to the present arterial drainage (introduced in the early 1900s).

Townlands
Ballyporeen
Béal Átha Póirín – Ford Mouth of (the) Little Hole, or of the Indigo. Area: 150 acres.
Póirín is the local name for the dye once used in quantity in a local tuck mill. On the main street is a pointed house where the immortal 'Wedding of Ballyporeen' was celebrated. Fairs were held on 12 May and 21 August.
Names of places within the townland:
> Bóthar an Adhmaid – Road of the Timber. It is the road leading to Lisfunshion from the village.

Coolagarranroe
Cúil a' Gharráin Ruaidh – Corner of the Red Grove. Area: 3,493 acres.
This, after Shanrahan, is the largest townland in the Decies.
Names of places within the townland:
> Knockeenatoung (perhaps Cnuicín na Tuinne) – Little Hill of the Shaking Bog.
> Cahergal Bridge (Cathair Gheal) – White Stones Fort.
> Sheep River.
> Gorteennacousha (Goirtín na Chabhra) – Little Garden of the Stepping Stones.
> Poulakerry (Poll a Choire) – Hole of the Cauldron.
> Mitchelstown Caves. The present well-known cave is a comparatively modern discovery. 'Desmond Cave', a quarter of a mile further west, has

been quite overlooked since the accidental discovery, in 1833, of its now-famous neighbour. The name 'Desmond Cave' derives from the capture, in Elizabeth's time, of the Súgan Earl by the White Knight. It is also known locally as Uaimh na Caorach Glaire – 'Cave of the Grey-Green Sheep'.

Uaimh na gCat – The (Wild) Cats Cave.

Sean Uaimh – Old Cave. Also known as Uaimh na Caorach Glaire – Cave of the Grey (or Light Green) Sheep.

Gleann na nGaibhlte – Little and Great Galtees.

Móin na bhFearnóg – Bog of the Alders.

Móinteán Uaithne – Green Little Bog.

Clair an Aifrinn – The Mass Trench.

Sráid na mBodach – Street of the Churls. A small sub-division of the townland.

Gleann na Gualann – Glen of the Shoulder. Another sub-division.

Gort a Chnuic – The Hill Garden.

The next six names apply to points on the Galtee mountains (west to east).

Ladhar Ruadh – Red River Fork

Cnoc na Ladhaire – Hill of the River Fork.

Cnoc na Scuaibe – Hill of the Broom

Bán Árd – High Field. A sub-division of the townland.

Cnoc na Láraidhe – Meaning uncertain. 'Láraidhe' may be the side rails of a cart.

Galtee Mountain. Na Gaibhte – Mountain Peaks. The ancient name was Sliabh gCrot – 'Mountain of the Small Harps'.

Skeheenarinky

Sceichín an Rince – The Dancing Bush. Area: 3,024 acres.

Names of places within the townland:

Breac-Bhán – Speckled Field. A sub-division of the townland and of a small stream which, having drained the sub-division, falls in the Funshion river.

Áth an Tighe Chrainn – Tree House Ford. A sub-division.

Seefin (Suidhe Finn) – Finn's Sitting Place. A cone-shaped mountain, 1,469ft high, on the western slope of which is Galtee Castle.

Barra Buidhe – Yellow (Hill) Summit. Another sub-division.

Tobar a Chinn – Well of the Head.

Bóthar Dubh – Black Road.

Páirc na Cille – Field of the Early Church. The site is indicated by a quadrangular mounded or untilled space called Cill Mhic Chairín (or

Mhic Oirín); Power records the site on the holding of a farmer named Quinlan.

Cnoc Riabhach – Grey Hill. It is near the north boundary of the townland.

Gort a'Chnuic – Garden of the Hill. A sub-division.

Árd na Sceiche – Height of the Whitethorn.

Clocha Breaca – Speckled Rocks.

Ladhracha – River Forks. It separates the townland from the neighbouring Coolagarranroe.

Tubbrid (Tiobraid Chiarán)

The origin of the parish goes back to the fifth century according to the *Life of St Declan*. St Declan, the apostle of the Decies, baptised the infant Ciaran at the well from which the future church and parish derived their name – Tiobraid Chiarán. The church ruin at Tubbrid possesses a peculiar interest; it is one of the few examples of a 17th century church of the people. It is a small, plain, rectangular building with a tablet over the door requesting prayers for Fr Eugene O'Duffy and Dr Geoffrey Keating, who caused the chapel to be built. O'Duffy was a Franciscan from Co. Cavan who wrote satires on two Protestant bishops, Miler McGrath and Mathew Shine. Tubbrid is also the burial place of Archbishop Brenan of Cashel, a bishop of Penal times.

Townlands

Clogheenafishoge

Cloichin na Fuireóige – Little Rock of the Lark. Area: 2,077 acres.

'Fuireóg' is a skylark, but here refers to a lady's name, Fuireóg Ní Longargáin, who is associated with a castle and whose memory still survives locally. The *cloichín* is a jutting platform of rock, upon which the castle stood.

Names of places within the townland:

Clair an Airgid – Trench of the Silver.

Móin a' Lín – Flax Bog. The name derives from a large pond found here in which flax was steeped.

Móin a'tSraoille – Bog of the Clown (or untidy person).

An Ladhairín – The Little River Fork.

Faill Dhearg – Red Cliff.

Kilcoran

Cill Chuaráin – Cuaran's Church. Area: 953 acres.

The church site is in a field on the north side of the road (N8). Close to the church site is a holy well, now dried up. The patron is presumably Cuaran

the Wise (Cuarán an Eaccna I nDéiribh Mumhan) whose feast day is 9 February.
Names of places within the townland:
  Móin na Mionnán – Bog of the Jacksnipes.
  Móin a'Leacht – Bog of the Monumental Pile (stones).
  Móin an Fheadáin – Bog of the Streamlet
  Cnoc an Chiaigh – Hill of the Fog.
  Cnoc Bán – White Hill.

Kilroe
  Coill Ruadh – Red-Coloured Wood. Area: 544 acres.
  Names of places within the townland:
    Cill Ghainimhe – Church of the Sand. An early church site, so named because of its proximity to a sand-pit.

Ballylooby
  Béal Átha Lúbaigh – Mouth of Looby's Ford.
  Ballylooby village is in the townland of Knockane (Cnocán).

Poulavaula
  Poll a'Mhála – Hole of the Bag. Area: 289 acres.

24

The Schools Folklore Collection

A COLLECTION of local folklore was compiled in Irish primary schools in 1937–39. The collection was made by getting pupils to write on a number of topics in copybooks. The topics included local traditions, stories, old cures and pishogues (superstitions), as well as oral history on themes such as the Great Famine. A project known as *dúchas*, which is based in the National Folklore Collection, University College Dublin, and includes the Schools Collection, aims to put the information online, but to date a very small percentage is available. Burncourt National School did not participate in the project; the information on the Burncourt area comes from the archive of material generated in the Skeheenarinky and Ballyporeen national schools. What follows is some of the topics that were covered.

Folk cures

It is not recommended that these are tried. The cures reflect traditions in the area from almost a hundred years ago and were taken down by pupils from interviews with older people in the district. The following is a synopsis of the folklore transcribed by the school children.

Toothache:
Put a frog in your mouth.
Drink mare's milk.
When a tooth falls out, kiss it, bless it and throw it over your head.
Camomile is a cure for sore teeth. Pluck off the daisies, or if not in bloom, the leaves may do. The blossoms are put in a saucepan, covered with water and left beside the fire for about fifteen minutes. The water is then put into the mouth for a few minutes. It is necessary that the water is hot. Keep rinsing your mouth until you feel better. The water must not be swallowed.

Backache:

Boil potatoes and, when they are hot, lie on them.

Anyone born on the first of the month can cure backache. The sick person should lie on his/her belly and the person who was born on the first of the month should walk on his/her back.

Sciatica:

A plant called '*garrdha*' is boiled for forty-eight hours and the juice is drunk.

Boils:

Boil water, put it in a bottle, empty the bottle and put the bottle on top of the boil.

The rough side of St Patrick's Leaf (the shamrock) is put on the boil to draw out the pus, and the smooth side is used for healing.

Burn:

Lick an '*archuachair*' (the meaning of this word is unclear) and then lick the burn.

Melt the wax of a blessed candle, mix it with unsalted hog's lard and apply it as a plaster.

Rub bread soda on the burn at once.

Put the white of an egg to a fresh burn.

Consumption:

Boil five or six dandelions, drink the juice and bury the leaves.

Warts:

Get a white or black snail, rub it on the warts and hang the snail on a hawthorn bush or whitethorn tree.

For every wart, put a stone in a purse or bag and leave it on the road, or at a four-crossroads, and the person who finds the purse will take the warts.

Get a penny and rub it on the warts, then throw it at a four-crossroads and the person who finds it will take your warts.

Steal a piece of meat from another house, rub the meat on the warts and bury it in manure. As the meat rots, the warts fade away.

When you see the new moon, stand steady, take off your cap and make the sign of the cross. Keep looking at the moon, then pick up what is under your right foot. This will cure warts.

Wash the warts in a hole of water that you find unexpectedly.

Rheumatism:

Pick a weed called yarrow, wash it well, cut up the stem, leaves and roots, and leave it steeping for a day or two in pure spring water. Simmer it for a couple of hours, strain it, add it to a glass of best whiskey (known as first-shot whiskey, which is not to be got in every public house). A wine glass of this mixture in water, taken three times a day, will act as a preventative as well as a cure for pains.

Rickets:

The third generation of a blacksmith has a cure for rickets.

Measles:

Boil little black marbles found in a field after a sheep in new milk (milk from a sheep who recently lambed) and give it to a child to remove the measles.

Thrush:

The godfather of a child should blow his breath on the mouth of the child.

The person who suffers from thrush should be brought to somebody who never saw their father; that person should blow his breath on the sore mouth on three mornings, before sunrise.

Vomiting:

Kill a chicken and place the skin inside the gizzard, roast it to ashes and mix it with milk and drink.

Whooping (chin) cough:

Drink milk that a ferret is unable to finish.

Drink donkey's or sheep's milk.

The child's godfather should steal a goat's ear and hang it around the neck of the child.

Get children to toss turf mould (the small pieces of turf that are shed from sods of turf).

Two people stand at either side of a donkey and hand the child across to one another to cure the child. Another way is to pass the child under the donkey's belly.

Ask the first man that you meet riding a white horse what the best cure is; whatever he says, give it to the child.

Cuts or scars:

A dog's lick.

Rub a cobweb or a *snaaherla* (or *snaahurlus* – meaning unclear; perhaps a plantain) on the cut to stop bleeding and cure the cut.

Use the woolly leaves of hedge woundwort, a weed, to dress the wound (it was very useful in olden days, and used instead of cotton-wool).

Bruises:

Use leeches, which feed on turf and water and can be found in the mountains.

If anyone has bruised blood, put a leech on it and keep it covered. After an hour or so, the blood goes. The leech is then burned.

Thorns:

Draw a fox's tongue over the thorn and it will extract it.

Poultices:

The St Patrick's Leaf will draw all matter (pus) from sores; the coarse side is used for drawing, the fine side for healing.

Get a root of comfrey, take the skin off, scoop out some of the root, put it in a rag and put it on the sore.

St Anthony's fire (wild fire):

This infection, which has an associated with skin rash, can be cured by 'Cahill's blood', or the blood of a black cat. Cahill's blood must be 'pure' in that both parents must be Cahills – the mother's maiden name must also be Cahill. J.F. Tehan, a teacher in Clogheen National School, wrote for the Schools Folklore Collection, in 1937, that he had seen a man called Thomas O'Connor from Garrymore cured of wild fire. Mr O'Connor's neck was covered with watery blisters. His neighbour, who was a pure Cahill, came along, having fasted the whole morning, cut his finger and rubbed the bleeding part of the blisters. When the disease was not arrested immediately, two Cahill brothers came the following morning and both rubbed the blood very vigorously on the affected parts. They had decided that one blood was not strong enough, as the disease was pretty advanced. Within the course of a few days after the double rubbing, the blisters disappeared.

Scurvy:

Boil a grass that grows in Lake Muscraighe on the Galtees, drink the juice and throw away the grass.

Sore eyes:

Bathe sore eyes in black tea or bathe them with your fasting spit.

Sore throat:

If a child has a sore throat, they should turn their left stocking inside out and put it around their throat for three days.

Foxgloves (no recipe was given).

Buchaillains (ragwort) and wood sorrel are cures for a sore throat.

Get the juice from 'snarl' grass and drink it.

Stomach trouble:

Get a dandelion root and, similar to the yarrow, wash it well, cut up the stem and roots, and leave it steeping for a day or two in pure spring water (it doesn't need whiskey like the rheumatism cure). A glass of this in a little boiling water is then taken, when fasting, every morning.

Whittle finger:

Dip your finger in boiling potato water.

Hold your finger under cow dung.

Yellow jaundice:
Boil snails in new milk and stir with an ash stick; when the milk is boiled, the snails are taken out and the milk is drunk three times a day.

Bed-wetting:
Boil a hay-mouse in milk, throw the mouse away and give the milk to the child before going to bed.

Worms in horses:
Give them thistles.

Miscellaneous:
Donkey's milk is good for a weak child.

Folklore

The following stories about Burncourt can be read online in the archive of the Schools Folklore Collection. The stories, edited and condensed here, were recounted by an older generation and taken down by pupils in the schools in 1937–38. The names of those recounting the tales is given ahead of each tale.

Burial
Mary Walshe (aged 87 in 1937)

There was an old woman living in Burncourt and she told a farmer man where to bury her when she died. When she died, the man dug the grave in the place where she said. On the day of her funeral, another man would not allow her to be buried there. There was a priest home on holidays who was a great friend of the old woman. He told the man to bury her in his own burying place. Every night after nine o'clock, a light used to be seen in the man's yard. At first the man did not take any notice of it. But after a few nights he got frightened. He went to the priest and told him the story. The priest told him to have a Mass offered in the house, and he did. After that it was not seen any more.

A woman died (near Ballyporeen) and a man coming out of her house around 11 p.m. was met by the woman's ghost. This happened on three nights in succession. The family went to the priest in Clogheen and he asked if the woman had been buried without her medals or scapulars around her neck. The family went to the graveyard and put the medals and scapulars on the grave. She never appeared again.

Danish hoard
Mary Walshe

It is said by old people that two crocks of gold were hidden in a field on the north side of the road between Skeheenarinky Schoolhouse Cross and

Mountain Lodge. It is said that the Danes hid it when running from Brian Boru after the Battle of Soloheadbeg (the battle was most likely Sulchóid, near Limerick Junction, which took place in AD 960 when the Vikings were defeated by Mahon [Mathgamain], King of the Dál Cais and brother of Brian Boru). People dug for the gold but could not find it.

Guarded by a pig

Pat Fitzgerald (died in 1936, aged 83)

One day a man went up a little bohereen (little road) at Cathair Geal Bridge. He was followed by a pig. He had a crock of gold under his arm and when he came down, the pig was not with him. The people said he buried the gold in Bun na Lyra, in the townland of Coolagarranroe, with the pig to guard it.

Guarded by a dead man

Pat Fitzgerald

Once a man was supposed to have been in possession of gold. His servant boy asked him to see the gold but the owner of the gold kept putting off the appointment. The owner told the servant he would show it to him on a certain day, but that the servant should guard it, dead or alive, until a black sheep in one of the fields was killed on the threshold of the door. The servant agreed to this; he thought he could kill the black sheep on the threshold and then take the gold. But the owner killed the servant and buried him with the gold. The owner of the gold died without revealing its whereabouts. One day, an old scholar came to the door begging. The householders told the scholar about the loss of the gold. He told them to kill the black sheep on the threshold. They did not want to believe him, but out of respect they did what he told them. At the first blow they heard a laugh; at the second blow they heard another laugh; at the third blow they cut the head clean off and they heard a loud laugh. They went to where they heard the laugh and found the gold.

Guarded by a headless horse

Michael Ryan

Con Crotty, a pupil in Skeheenarinky school wrote down a story he heard from his great grand uncle, Michael Ryan. Michael Ryan dreamt three nights in a row that a crock of gold was under a whitethorn bush on the Black Road. On the fourth night he got a bottle of holy water and went to the place where he thought the gold was. He sprinkled the holy water around in a ring and began to dig inside the ring. He dug about five feet and he struck the pot. He heard a noise and he thought the Galtees were falling down on him. He looked up and saw a white headless horse running around the ring of holy water. He stopped digging and the horse vanished. The man went home. When the landowner got up in the morning and saw the hole in the bank, he was surprised and filled it in. Ten years after, a big flood came and swept away the bank and it is said the crock was taken in the flood. The landowner drowned one night when going across a field on a dark night.

The caves
Patrick Williams (aged 50 in 1937)

The Grey Sheep Cave is near Mitchelstown Caves in Coolagarranroe. Very many generations ago, an old Irish poet went into the cave and crossed the magic stream, which is in the cave, and he turned into a grey sheep. Years after, a shepherd went into the cave on May Day, crossed the stream and never came out. The shepherd happened to have a flute with him, and as he could not come out, he began playing a lament on the flute, hoping someone would hear him and come to his help. The people heard him but would not cross the stream to him. Often on May Day since the lamentation of the lost shepherd, the music of his flute can be heard in the cave underground. The Grey Sheep Cave is also called the Desmond Cave, because here the Fitzgerald known as the Sugán Earl was captured and betrayed by his kinsman, the White Knight of Kilbehenny.

A serpent in the lake
Pat Walshe

In the lake of Muscrcuighe (Lake Muskry), in the Galtee Mountains, there is said to be a serpent that St Patrick placed in the lake and promised he would free on Easter Sunday morning. When Easter Sunday morning came, the serpent rose to the surface of the lake and said 'Ta Domhnac na Cársa abhrad úaim a Pádraig' ('Patrick, this is the Passover Sunday for me'). One time, a landlord named Count Moore from Tipperary town visited the lake with his friends. They brought a boat to sail the lake and measure the depth. They got a rope with lead on the end, but every time they let it down, it was cut in two. They left for home and decided to come back another day with a number of men in order to drain the lake. As they started to drain it, they saw their homes were on fire. They went quickly to their homes, but there was nothing the matter; they said they would never again interfere with the lake.

Another version of this story is that a mysterious creature lives in one of the lakes on Galtymore and the monster puts its head over the water every seven years. Anyone or anything that happens to be near it falls into the lake. Once a crowd set out to visit the lake, bringing a man who was offered £100 to dive in. When he returned, he said he saw something like a stack of wheels. He was offered another £100 to examine the phenomenon but never returned to the surface.

Fairy sheep comes to farmer
Mary Walshe

A man named Gorman of Coolagarranroe lived where the Mulcahys of the caves live. At the time, it was the custom to kill something for Michaelmas night. There was a cave in Mr English's land called the old cave. A black sheep came out of this cave and grazed on Gorman's land, having lambs each year. Mr Gorman was going to kill one of the lambs for Michaelmas night, but when he went out to catch one of them, the mother of the flock bleated three times and she ran into the cave with her flock. She never came out again.

Hedge schools
John Moloney (aged 67 in 1937)

There was an old school house where John Walsh lived in the 1930s. A tall man who was blind in one eye taught the children there. The children made up his pay for him; each child gave him 5s. a quarter (in today's equivalent £20 or €22). All the children in the district went to school and the subjects were arithmetic, reading, writing, catechism, but not Irish. He was a very popular man, wearing a Caroline hat (a type of beret) and knee breeches. It is said that he was teaching until he was 84 years of age.

William O'Neill (aged 64 in 1937)

There was a school in a cow-house at Ard na Sgeithe, a townland in Skeheenarinky. The teacher taught reading and writing in Irish and English. The pupils gave him a cut of tobacco every week and sometimes a shilling (in today's equivalent £4 or €4.50). The teacher left after a time and never came back. O'Neill also told of a second hedge school in Tom Fitzgerald's house which was used at night and where Latin and 'sums' (arithmetic) were taught.

An unidentified pupil recorded a school at McGrath's Cross in Skeheenarinky that was an open-air school.

Food long ago
The following are records made in the Schools Folklore Collection on food topics.

Long ago people used to eat potatoes three times a day and drink 'ropy' milk (sticky milk). A servant boy or girl would have salt with the potatoes and a farmer and his family would drink milk. They had no cups or saucers and drank the milk out of peggins (piggins), which were timber vessels with a handle and 4in (10cm) in height.

An account of typical daily meals was recorded by a pupil in Skeheenarinky National School, based on the recollection of a Mrs English, who was 50 years old in 1937. She recounted that, in olden times, three meals a day consisted of equal parts yellow meal and oatmeal for breakfast, which was taken with a peggin of thick milk. The dinner was a big pot of potatoes which was placed on a table, on a cloth made from a bag. The potatoes were peeled with fingers, because there were no forks or knives. Everyone got a peggin of milk. Supper was the same as dinner. Whatever food was left over was put by the side of the fire so that the good people (fairies) would come at night and eat them.

The following is a list of food items, including information on how they were made and consumed.

Starch from potatoes:

The old people used to make starch from potatoes. They made a grater from the cover of a polish box by punching the lid with a nail and making about sixty holes. The rough side was used to grate the potatoes. The 'bruss' (broken bits) of the potato was boiled and the water was then strained. The 'bruss' was cooled for an hour and that made the starch.

Bread:

Three kinds of bread were made in the area: oatmeal, potato cake and soda bread. Bread was baked on one day and eaten over the course of a week. The bread was baked in a bastable (three-legged pot) over an open fire. A firebrand was used to hold the bastable or griddle; it was an iron circle or triangle with three legs which was placed on top of the fire and the griddle or bastable was set up on top.

Potato cake:

Potato cake was made by boiling potatoes, breaking them up as fine as flour and mixing through some flour, salt and bread soda. The ingredients were then mixed with milk and baked in a griddle. One record of the recipe includes fried fat bacon. A stand on three legs was placed on the fire and the griddle was put on top of the stand. Another account states that the potato cakes were baked in a bastable and served hot with gravy. The flour was made from wheat and oats, and was ground on Fridays at Walpole's in Cahir and Kilfinane.

Oaten bread:

In olden times, bread was made mainly from oats, as wheat was scarcely grown. The bread was made from oatmeal made into porridge, left to get cold and mixed by kneading with flour and milk. The mark cut on top of a cake was a cross, which was supposed to be lucky as it was first made by St Brigid. The Christmas cake was made from barm. Barm was made by mixing boiled peeled potatoes and water. This was put into a big jar and left by the fire for two to three days.

Pancakes:

Pancakes were made on St Bridget's night.

Sweet cakes:

The ingredients were currants, raisins, caraway seeds, barm and butter, and were eaten around Christmas.

Gránsacáin:

This was wheat boiled in a pot and mixed with sugar.

Blood pudding:

'Blood pudding' was a special kind of food which was filled with a mix of fatty meat, oatmeal, new milk, salt and pepper. The puddings were cleaned with cold water and filled with the mixture. The puddings were hung on a stick and part of them was placed in a pot of boiling water; they were boiled for an hour. They were prodded with a needle to prevent them from bursting.

Fish:

Fish were eaten on Fridays and bought from a van which came from Dungarvan.

Meat:

Meat was expensive and ordinary people could not afford to buy it. It was eaten around Christmas.

Eggs:

Eggs were only eaten during Easter.

Tea:

This was expensive; it was drank at Christmas and Easter. The tea cost 10*s.* per lb (equivalent to €25). One child wrote that when the people drank tea, they drank gallons of it.

Lent

On certain days of Lent, bread made with milk was not eaten and milk was not put in tea.

Making butter

Butter was made at home on the farm before the creamery mass-produced butter. A certain day was set-aside in the household for making or churning butter. The milk vessels (churns) were made of oak and were known as 'cans'.

The cow's milk was poured from the cans and left to rest in tin-pans or wooden keelers, which were put on a high frame on four legs (a 'stilling'). The milk was left to stand for about one day, until the cream came to the top. The cream was then poured into a cream tub. The cream was skimmed off with a wooden plate known as a 'skimmer'. Cream was collected over four to five days. The woman of the house got her churning barrel ready and then poured the cream into the barrel, which was turned until the butter was made.

There appears to have been three types of butter churns. One type was a dash-churn, which had a handle or 'churn staff' at both sides; these were used to twist the barrel and churn the butter. Two bars, known as 'dashers', at the bottom of the churn helped churn the milk to make butter. The second type was a barrel-churn, about five feet (1.52m) high, round and narrow at the top, with a timber lid. The lid had a hole; a timber stick (known as a 'beater') went through the hole and was used to beat the cream into butter. The third type was an 'end-over-end' butter churn, which had a glass lid that allowed the butter to be seen as it was made.

Butter-making took about half an hour. When the butter was made, a spicket was used to draw off the buttermilk. The butter was then taken from the churn and put in a large tub; spring water was then poured over the butter. The butter was patted with a 'butter spade' (butter pats) or 'skimmer', and all excess buttermilk was removed. Salt was then added and mixed through.

The butter was then put in a firkin, or lidded bucket, and was ready to be eaten or sold. Some farmers combined the butter with that of his neighbour and they sold it together. Butter was also stored for four to five weeks so that it was sold in bulk and made a 'nice bit of money', as recounted by James Ruarke in the Schools Folklore Collection. The price of butter was about eight or nine old pence per pound. Farmers often had six or seven firkins for sale at the same time. Each firkin weighed 56lbs (25.4kg). Butter from Skeheenarinky, and perhaps Burncourt, was brought to markets in Mitchelstown, Clonmel and Kilfinane, Co. Limerick, where merchants bought the butter. The merchants in Mitchelstown were Mr Hayes and Mr Hanrahan.

Making flour

An account by one pupil in Skeheenarinky National School recorded a small mill in Carroll's farm in Bán Árd townland in Burncourt. Wheat was brought to the mill to be ground for flour. There were other mills in Clogheen; they were owned by Grubbs and Fennells.

Flour was made by grinding wheat and the by-products were coarse and fine bran and tailings. Oats produced oatmeal. Some people used querns to grind the oats. The querns were made of one big, flat stone and another similar stone.

The oats were ground between the stones. A description in the Folklore Collection records a second type of quern that was like a little table with four timber legs. Part of the table was made for holding the grain. There were two rollers in front with a handle attached. The grain was put into the part of the table used for holding the grain. One hand held the handle and the other pushed the grain into the rollers. The grain was put through several times, until it was made into fine flour.

Setting the potatoes

When a woman cut the potatoes, she used a short, narrow, pointed knife. She sat on a small stool, caught two or three small potatoes and put two or three cuts in them. She left an eye in every *sciolán* (seed potato) because it was out of the eye that the stalk came. The piece where there was no eye was called a 'cruit'. The woman put the sciolán into one bag and the cruits into another. Some people added lime to the bag of sciolán two days before they were set.

In past times men formed a *meitheal* (neighbours joined together to deal with harvest) to help each other when setting and digging potatoes. Dung was scattered on the potato garden and lime was added to the soil. The withered grass was sometimes burnt off the field before making potato ridges. A mixture of cow-dung, clay and grass was called a 'troc' and was added as fertiliser. Ridges were made with spades known as 'bawn spades'. The ridges were made of two sods; a sod was dug at each side and laid over the ground between the dug sods to form a ridge. Four men were able to dig an Irish acre of bawn (untilled ground) in a day. Tom Durney of Cahergeal made a timber plough and used an old spade to make the plough-sock, and this was used to make ridges and plough the furrows. Potatoes were set into three holes made across the ridges and the holes were closed by a boy using a 'cronín'. The potatoes were earthed up to encourage stalk growth. Potatoes were harvested in one day by a *meitheal*.

Oats

Oats were set on ridges and harvested with hooks. Two men would cut one ridge.

Making hay

A *meitheal* was formed to save the hay. The hay was brought into the haggart (a small field) and made into a large cock, or reek, of hay. The farmer's wife would then make a good dinner of potatoes, meat and cabbage, and, if possible, she had a peggin of buttermilk to serve to each man. A man was dispatched to the public house to get porter in a measure known as a 'half-tierce' (which was a cask or vessel that held twenty-one wine gallons – or about ninety-five litres). A girl was sent to the neighbours to get the young girls and women to come to a dance in the evening. Tea and sweet cake were served at the dance. The stout was put into the barn and the farmer reddened a poker to tap the half-tierce; the stout was then drawn off into a large bucket and each man was given two saucepans of stout. Mick Carroll recalled for the Schools Folklore Collection that the girls arrived with 'bright smiling faces, wearing shawls and with their long hair plaited and fixed to suit their complexion. At that time girls used no lipstick. They had far better health and looked much better than girls in 1937'. When supper was over, music was played on a fiddle or concertina and set-dancing included quad drills, gallops, reels and hornpipes. There was a break mid-way through the dance where the men took more stout and the ladies went to the parlour to have wine and cake with the woman of the house. The dance would break up at dawn and people travelled home in horse-drawn carts.

Weather
Country people observed nature, including animal behaviour to foretell the weather.

Signs of Rain:
A frog comes into a house. Swallows fly low. Crows gather in great numbers. Crows fly low and fast. Crows go to the ditches for shelter. A dog eats grass. Farm stock cluster around the ditches. A horse turns its back to the ditch. Geese call. When a curlew calls. Large numbers of insects lodge on the road. When you see a pissmyer (ant). The hens pick themselves. Midges are out at night. Crickets sing. Ants fly. The cat turns its back to the fire. A cat washes behind its ears. When spaniels sleep and spiders from their cobwebs creep. Wind from the west and from the south. Fog in the morning. A thick fog on an August morning. Rows of cloud in the sky at night. The image of a fire can be seen through a window. A pale or coppery sunset. A red colour in the sky after dawn. Sun rising early in the morning. One or two rainbows. A ring around the moon. When the fire is blue. The smoke curls around the chimney. The hills seem nearer. When the clouds come down the hill. Bubbles in the water. Dry soot falls down the chimney. Dust clears off the road. The moon is on its back. When sparks remain on the kettle.
Signs of frost:
The sky is red before the sun sets. The sun is red or coppery when it sets. The stars are very near each other. The stars shine bright. The sky is red before the sun sets. A star falls. Dark and red clouds. Wind comes from the north or east. Streams can be heard running at night.

Signs of thunder:
The sun is coppery before noon. The sky becomes black on a warm day. A rainbow at night.

Signs of a storm:
The crows fly low. Sheep come down from the mountain. Cattle go for shelter to the ditches. Seagulls fly inland. Coppery clouds. Nearly all the stars are covered by cloud. A ring around the moon. The rainbow encircles the earth with a second rainbow behind. The moon is on its back. The rising moon is red. The sky is dark red at sunset. Smoke blows downwards. The wind blows from the south-east.

Signs of snow:
A cat with its back to the fire. The wind blows from the north or north-east. A dog eats grass. Birds come to the door. Smoke blows straight up. The dust rises out of the road. The clouds are like ridges. Sheep gather together on the hill.

Signs of fine weather:
The sky is red in the east before dawn. A ring around the sun. The moon is straight. When you hear the sound of a river on a wet night. Dust on the road. Smoke goes up straight. Fog on the hill. A rainbow in the evening. Swallows fly high. The crane flies north. A sore nose.

Pishogues

Many of the pishogues are centred on butter-making. Most of the stories in the Schools Folklore Collection recount the failure to make butter because of a pishogue, or bad luck charm, on the farm. The priest was often called to break the charm. One woman couldn't get the butter made and the churn was full of foam. She called the priest, who read prayers over the churn, and the butter was then made. The woman searched her farm and found a calf's leg buried on a boundary ditch (the calf's leg was buried by a person who wanted bad luck brought to the woman's household). She was told to burn the leg. Another woman was sick and she asked her neighbours to churn milk for butter for her. They churned all day but could not make the butter. The sick woman got up and stirred something in a cup and threw it into the churn and the butter was made.

Another account relates how a person whose butter 'was gone' (couldn't be made) could go to Mass and borrow a sheaf of oats. This ensured that butter could again be made on the farm. Throwing a 'glugger' (a '*gliogar*' or infertile egg; this egg was left behind when the rest hatched and by that time it was rotten) into another man's farm 'took the butter' – the household were unable to churn the butter. In a certain house where butter could not be made, blood appeared on the churns. A Mass was offered in the house and the priest told the farmer to put the plough share in the fire – the man making the pishogues would come for the plough share. The next-door neighbour arrived during the Mass for the plough share and after that the farmer could make the butter. A separate story recounts how people found butter plastered to the walls of the hay shed or cow house. Butter could not be made after that.

Food that was misplaced or misused was another signal for bad luck. Meat, eggs and butter were buried on the land and the cows and calves died. Bad eggs were left in the hen-house and the hens didn't lay. Meat was put in cow-houses or in the field and this took the milk from the farmer. Milk was put in bottles to take the calves (the calves died).

Other bad-luck omens:
- It was bad luck to meet a grey horse very early in the morning. It was good luck to find a horse-shoe.
- Giving out money on a Monday, as you would be paying out money for the rest of the week.
- If a cock crowed at the door it was a sign of death.
- If a person taking water from a well for a churn got the water first, he could prevent another person from churning butter.

May Eve
May Eve was a time on the farm when witchcraft could be practised to bring bad luck to neighbours. The bad luck was warded off by sprinkling holy water or Easter water, or lighting fires to purify the land and destroy any evil. Holy water was thrown on crops and animals to stop the neighbours from making pishogues (charms). Farmers dug a sod from each corner of the field and put the holy water under the sod. Some people stayed up all night to mind the cows; if a sup of milk was taken on May Eve or May Day, all the milk would be taken too. The following are stories about May Eve that were recorded by children in Skeheenarinky National School.
- A man found eggs at the end of every ridge he was digging. Sometime after, all the fowl died and he was unable to make butter.
- Hen and duck eggs found in the 'wynds' of hay (haystacks) meant that the crops would not grow well, while those of the person who put them there would grow very well.
- Dead hens and calves were thrown into fields and some of the landowner's hens and calves died. The other hens stopped laying.
- A man was caught milking his neighbour's cows. He was brought to the guards and tried in court, where he got six months. That finished the

pishogues in the locality.

- A man digging his garden found a buried cow's head. The next day one of his best cows was dying. He brought her in, but she died; within two days, two more cows also died.
- A cure for a curse was to rub a sup of milk on the cow's back and then take the piece of hair that was rubbed with the milk; this would enable you to take someone else's milk.
- If you saw someone about to take water from a churn, you could take it before them and then take their butter.
- A man had ten young calves but each died in succession. The farmer got the vet and he found the calves had no signs of disease. The farmer found rotten eggs and a calf's leg in a bag buried where he fed the calves. The man who worked the pishogue died barking like a bulldog and eating his own flesh.

May Morning

May Morning (Lá Bealtaine) was the beginning of summer and an important time in the countryside. Similar to May Eve, there were some customs which were followed to ward off evil or bad luck.

Farmers used to light a fire on 1 May and make the cows jump over it to prevent bad luck during the year. Farmers also lit a fire at the four corners of the farm to keep the devil out for the year.

A man who travelled regularly from Skeheenarinky to Tipperary town usually set off at about four o'clock in the morning. Once the man set off at the usual time and came to a river; he was about to cross it at an áth (a fording place) when he saw a woman with a skimmer (a wooden saucer for skimming milk) skimming the water near the stepping stones as if it were milk. She put the water into two buckets. She didn't hear him coming and he said '*Leath de sin agamsa*' (give me half of that). She caught the two buckets and ran away before he knew who she was. The next day, when he churned the butter, he had twice as much.

The Hare connection

Many of the stories of pishogues are connected to women turning themselves into a hare. Some old women pretended that they were gifted with witchcraft and told innocent people that they could take the butter or milk from their neighbours, or increase the amount of milk from the cows. The women were paid with bags of potatoes, pieces of bacon, a bottle of whiskey and a few round pieces of silver. The following are some of the stories recorded by children in Skeheenarinky School in 1937.

A man was hunting one May morning and he saw a hare between the cows and fired a shot. He knocked the hare but it rose again and ran to the farmer's house. The door was locked but the hare got in the window. The man looked in the window and saw a woman sitting on a chair with blood all around her.

A man went for his cows one morning and he saw a hare amongst them. He put the dog after the hare and the hare ran into a hole in a cabin wall. As the hare was going in, the dog caught it by the leg. The hare was a woman making pishogues; after the dog caught her, she spent a month in bed.

Pattern in Ballysheehan
A pattern day was a celebration of a local saint and usually took place at an old church site or a holy well. The pattern included prayers as well as festivities such as music, dancing and sometimes alcohol was taken. The pattern day in Ballysheehan celebrated the local saint, Laishrén.

Some men were coming home from the pattern day in Ballysheehan and they started to fight outside a man's house. The man came out to make peace between them and they killed him. Water then sprung up from the spot where he died and sometimes, at certain times of the year, blood. One night a girl was going home from a dance and she saw a man wearing a white cloak and holding a lighted candle crossing the road.

Another story about Ballysheehan was related by Maurice Fitzgerald of Skeheenarinky, recollecting how the pattern day in Ballysheehan was an enjoyable day. Once, people recognised two brothers of Betty Ní Bhroin's (the outlaw Willie Brenan's brothers) and fought them. When Betty heard this, she went to Ballysheehan, where she 'struck right and left until she and her brothers cleared the whole place'.

Dance in Rehill
A dance was held at a place called 'The Old Round'. One evening, as the boys and girls were dancing, a strange man came to the dance and asked a girl to dance; the girl was the prettiest girl at the dance. The stranger took the girl up in the air and out of sight. She later appeared to a man and told him not to say to anyone that he ever heard or saw Glogh-na-luba ('the cry of a witch'). There was never a dance held in that place again.

The lough
According to tradition, Skeheenarinky got the name from the lough. There was a green patch in the middle of the lough and a *sceach* (bush) grew there. As the surface was not firm, the water underneath made the bush bob up and down and so the name 'the dancing bush' (Skeheenarinky) was taken from the bush.

The lough dried up about a hundred years ago and local people got bog oak from the lake bed, which was used as mantles over the fireplaces. A man drowned in the lough in the late 1890s and a ditch was built around the lough for safety.

Clever fox

There are various accounts in the Schools Folklore Collection of how foxes showed their intelligence.

One account, from Pat Fitzgerald of Skeheenarinky, related how a fox was chased by horsemen and hounds. It was unable to climb the gate and went for the stile. A farmer was sitting on the stile and didn't allow the fox to pass over. The fox dropped to the ground. When the hounds were within a hundred yards (90m) the fox looked pitifully at the farmer, who relented and let the fox pass. The fox escaped. The next morning the farmer saw the fox guiding three ducks and tipping them with its tail. The farmer couldn't find an owner for the ducks so he kept them. This was how the fox showed its gratitude.

Another story, told by Jim Scully, was of a fox who took a hen from Tom Durney's farm every day. Tom Durney and Bill Walsh watched out for the fox and the fox saw them so he went to Bill Walsh's and took a hen from there.

A fox was caught in a trap and was beaten with a stick by a landowner. The fox pretended to be dead and, when the man left, the fox got up and ran off.

A farmer came out to his yard and saw all the geese were dead in the geese-house, as well as a fox. The farmer got a pike and threw the fox out on a dung heap. When the fox saw he was safe, he ran off.

Hunting the wren

There was an old tradition of hunting the wren on St Stephen's Day. The wren was followed along the ditches and in the holly trees on Christmas Day and caught. A holly bush was cut down in preparation for hunting the wren. On St Stephen's Day ribbons were tied to the holly bush and the wren was tied on top. Those following the wren went from house to house, singing, playing mouth-organs and dancing, and the householders threw out a few pence.

25

Irish Words and Phrases in Use in the Area in the 1930s

THESE FOLLOWING words were recorded in the Schools Folklore Collection and were in common usage. The area around Burncourt was recorded in the 1901 Census; many of the inhabitants were listed as bilingual, speaking both Irish and English. Irish was taught in primary schools for one hour per day from 1922 and, as it was spoken at home, most must have learned it outside of school, too. Some words continue to be used in the area and reflect an older dialectic tradition.

Amadán: A fool (male).

Angiséor: A miserable person.

Ath: Shallow water (a ford in the river).

Bacach: A lame person or hindrance.

Báinín: Home-spun cloth or a white waistcoat.

Balbháinín: Half-deaf.

Baolín: A small round box.

Bata Buile: A stick used to close the door at night.

Breall: To sulk.

Beart: A bundle ('a beart of hay').

Bogán: An egg without a shell.

Borán: Dried dung (used as fuel).

Boreen: A road.

Bothán: A shack or old house; a shelter.

Bothanach: Rambling from house to house, or visiting.

Brurna: A little bunch.

Buailtcán: A flail or blackthorn stick.

Bucán: A door hinge.

Búracín: The hasp of a half-door.

Ceannas: To tie a cow's leg to her head (to stop her going through ditches).

Carraig: A rock.

Céol: Music.

Cioráns: Sods of turf.

Ciotóg: Left-handed.

Claipineach: A man without feet.

Clánín: A thing for edging a scythe.

Clerí: A hook (?) Hung on the wall.

Codrálcí: Talking foolish.

Culactín: The bottom of a dresser where hens were kept (in the kitchen).

Crúbín: A pig's foot.

Croigthín: A stocking without a vamp.

Crudgín: A small, stout stick used for washing.

Crunáning: Grumbling.

Crusheen: Pot or jug.

Cuairdeach: Visiting to play cards.

Cuiseog: A stick used for washing potatoes; the stick had a knob ('a *gruipín*') on one end.

Donnsa: A stupid person; a dunce.

Drib: Dirty water.

Dromach: A backband (horse or donkey harness).

Dúg: A cup of water.

Dúidín: A clay pipe, or smoking; with a broken stem and usually smoked by a woman.

Dúirnins: The handle of a scythe.

Fagharcán: A knot.

Fialthaín: A glen.

Fionnánach: Withered grass.

Gabháil: A bundle ('go out for a *gabháil* of sticks').

Gabhlóg: A fork for cutting turf; a timber fork used to hold bushes back while cutting back the stems.

Gailseach: An earwig.

Gamail: A child.

Garsún: A young boy.

Gead: A twig.

Gibris: Foolish talk.

Gile: A child.

Giobal: A rag.

Glugaoil: Gurgling.

Glugar: A bad egg.

Gob: A mouth.

Goblachán: One jaw bigger than the other.

Gor (or cré soileach): Cleanings of the bog brought into the yard and shovelled until rotten, then mixed with dung for potatoes (also called troc).

Grád-mo-croide: Soft talk.

Grouncánaige: Grumbling (grousing).

Grug: Heels ('sitting on your *grug*').

Gunach: Hemp.

Lún scar: Crawling.

Leaca: A hilly field.

Leana: A child.

Leisce: Lazy.

Loctin: A loft.

Lúidín: A small finger.

Málín: A bag for setts (seed potatoes), or a nose-bag used to feed a horse.

Meitheal: A bunch of men working.

Míadbharac: A miserable fellow.

Mí-ádh: Bad luck.

Óinseach: A fool (female).

Piscín: A kitten.

Plámas: Fake talk, or flattery.

Preacaill: A sulk.

Puícín: Blinkers (put over the eyes).

Pus: A face.

Riocareacht: Shivering.

Roraire: A rogue.

Sálíní: The heels of a cart – where the shafts stick out at the back of the cart.

Sálog: The ashes left in a pipe; the butt of tobacco ashes left in a pipe.

Scabaróir (scaróg): A miser.

Scagún: An ignorant fellow.

Scalp: An old house with a bad roof.

Scathamh: Awhile (wait awhile).

Scathán: A furze bush.

Sceach: A thorn bush.

Scilléad: A small pot; a skillet.

Sciolláin (sceaoleáns): Seed potatoes (setts).

Scoraidheact: Visiting.

Sculóg: A small little man.

Sealtán: A glen.

Seardán: Noisy breathing.

Shlán: A spade for cutting turf.

Shulla: A gust of wind.

Sibhaine: A fairy.

Sí-gaoithe: Fairy wind.

Sneachta Séidean: Windy snow.

Sop: A small bundle.

Spailpín; A journeyman or travelling labourer (a spade man).

Speanach: Roots of burnt heath.

Striall: A streel; an untidy person.

Subadán: Stubble.

Sugán: A chair made of straw.

Taoibín: A patch on a shoe.

Taobans: The timbers under the rafters (similar to slate laths).

Tranín: Long grass.

Taoscán: A small bit.

Trí-na-céile: Mixed-up.

Tuillí: A treader on a spade; a step on the side of a spade for cutting turf.

Túnínte: A game played where two boys caught each other by the hand and leg; two other boys did the same and they struck into each other.

Túrtóg: A height.

References

Bassett, G.H., *County Tipperary 100 Years Ago: A Guide and Directory 1889* (Belfast: Friar's Bush Press, 1889).

Bric, M.J., 'The Whiteboy Movement in Tipperary, 1760–80' in D.W. Nolan and T. McGrath (eds), *Tipperary: History and Society* (Dublin: Geography Publications, 1985).

Butler, D.J., *South Tipperary, 1570–1841: Religion, Land and Rivalry* (Dublin: Four Courts Press, 2006).

Conry, M.J., *Picking Bilberries, Fraocháns and Whorts in Ireland: The Human Story* (Carlow: Michael J. Conry, 2011).

Cleary, R.M., *Ballysheehan Church and Graveyard* (Privately published, 2001).

Cleary, R.M., *Burncourt National School* (Privately published, 2006).

Cleary, R.M., 'Burncourt Castle Excavations', *North Munster Antiquarian Journal*, vol. 48, pp. 63–105.

De Falco, K., 'Ellen Conway – Single Mother' in J. O'Neill, K. De Falco, M. Caulfield and B. Ryan (eds), *Daughters of Dún Iascaigh* (Cahir: Cahir Women's History Group, 2018).

Everard, R.H.A.J., 'The family of Everard, I', *The Irish Genealogist*, vol. 7, 3, pp. 328–48.

Everard, R.H.A.J., 'The family of Everard, II', *The Irish Genealogist*, vol. 7, 4, pp. 505–42.

Flanagan, M., *Ordnance Survey Letters containing information relative to the Antiquities of the County of Tipperary. Collected during the progress of the Ordnance Survey in 1840*, vol. 1.

Hallinan, M., 'The capture and execution of District Inspector Potter' in M. Hallinan (ed.), *Tipperary County: People and Places* (Dublin: Kincora Press, 1993).

Lewis, S., *A Topographical Dictionary of Ireland* (London: S. Lewis & Co.,

1837).

McGrath, M., 'Statement by Maurice McGrath', Bureau of Military History, 1913–21. Document No. W.S. 1701.

Murphy, T.A., 'Father Nicholas Sheehy, P. P., Clogheen' in M. Hallinan (ed.), *Tipperary County: People and Places*. (Dublin: Kincora Press, 1993).

O' Brien, W., *Christmas on the Galtees: an inquiry into the condition of the tenantry of Mr Nathaniel Buckley by the special correspondent of the 'Freeman's Journal'* (Dublin: The Central Tenants' Defence Assoc., 1878).

Olden, M., 'Geoffrey Keating – Seathrún Céitinn: Tipperary Priest and Scholar' in M. Hallinan (ed.), *Tipperary County: People and Places* (Dublin: Kincora Press, 1993).

Ordnance Survey Letters relating to the first Ordnance Survey of Co. Tipperary (1839).

Marnane, D.G., *The 3rd Brigade: A History of the Volunteers/IRA in South Tipperary 1913–21* (Tipperary: Tipperary County Library Service, 2018).

O'Riordan, E., *Famine in the Valley* (Privately published, 1995).

O'Riordan, E., *Lonely Little God's Acre: A History of Shanrahan Church* (Tipperary: Galty Cottage Books, 2012).

O'Riordan, E., *The Case of Fr Nicholas Sheehy* (Tipperary: Galty Cottage Books, 2014).

O'Shea, J., *Priest, Politics and Society in Post-famine Ireland* (Dublin: Wolfhound Press, 1983).

Power, P., *The Place-Names of Decies* (London: Nutt, 1907).

Power, P., *A Bishop of Penal Times: Being Letters and Reports of John Brenan Bishop of Waterford (1671–93) and Archbishop of Cashel (1677–93)* (Cork: Cork University Press, 1930).

Power, P.C., *History of South Tipperary* (Cork: Mercier Press, 1989).

Power, T.P., *Land, Politics and Society in Eighteenth-Century Tipperary* (Oxford: Oxford University Press, 1997).

Ryan, T., 'Statement by Thomas Ryan', Bureau of Military History, 1913–21. Document No. W.S. 785.

Simington, R.C. (ed.), *The Civil Survey AD 1654–1656 County of Tipperary, Vol. 1* (Dublin: Dublin Stationery Office, 1931).

Smyth, W.J., *Map-Making, Landscapes and Memory: A Geography of Colonial and Early Modern Ireland c. 1530–1750* (Cork: Cork University Press, 2006).

Smyth, W.J., 'Estate records and the making of the Irish landscape: An example from County Tipperary', *Irish Geography*, vol. 9, 1, pp. 29–49.

Ua Cearnaigh, S., 'Kit Conway – Hero of Jarma', *Irish Democrat*.

Notes

1. Dawson's Table was named after J.H. Massey Dawson, an estate owner in the Glen of Aherlow.
2. Willie Brennan was a highwayman who robbed from the rich and gave to the poor; he was executed in Clonmel in 1804 or 1812.
3. These are stones which have a depression in the centre and are frequently near ancient churches or monasteries. The stones are usually filled with rainwater and seen as either curing or cursing stones.
4. The date of 1649 should be 1650. There was a change from the Roman to the Gregorian calendar in 1650 and this resulted in this anomaly.
5. Information from B. Cunningham lecture, Duhill, August 2019.
6. Oliver Plunkett was canonised in 1975.
7. Burke's account of Fr Sheehy's trial is presented in Ed O'Riordan's book *The case of Fr Nicholas Sheehy* (2014).
8. The correct spelling is Colclough (rather than Coakley) as the name comes from the shooting of Henry Colclough in 1923. Colclough had taken over a farm from which William Galvin had been evicted.
9. Ms Dobbins lived across the road from Creed's shop and the house is now demolished.
10. Bureau of Military History, 1913–21.
11. A list compiled by Neil Donovan, Ballyporeen, on the basis of pension records included Jeremiah, Tim and Thomas Luddy, Tim, John, Patrick and Morgan Mulcahy, David, Owen, Patrick and Thomas Connors, Thomas and William English, Denis and William Riordan, Patrick and Thomas Boran, John and James O'Donoghue, Patrick Quinlan, John and Michael Cagney, Patrick Fox and John Flynn.
12. Everard Patent documents are lists of landholdings within the Everard estate.